Quantitative Applications in the Social Sciences

A SAGE PUBLICATIONS SERIES

Quantitative Applications in the Social Sciences

A SAGE PUBLICATIONS SERIES

Series/Number 07–149

QUANTILE REGRESSION

LINGXIN HAO
The Johns Hopkins University

DANIEL Q. NAIMAN
The Johns Hopkins University

For information:

Sage Publications, Inc.
2455 Teller Road
Thousand Oaks, California 91320
E-mail: order@sagepub.com

Sage Publications Ltd.
1 Oliver's Yard
55 City Road
London EC1Y 1SP
United Kingdom

Sage Publications India Pvt. Ltd.
B 1/1 1 Mohan Cooperative Industrial Area
Mathura Road, New Delhi 110 044
India

Sage Publications Asia-Pacific Pte. Ltd.
33 Pekin Street #02-01
Far East Square
Singapore 048763

Printed in the United States of America.

Library of Congress Cataloging-in-Publication Data

Hao, Lingxin, 1949–
Quantile regression / Lingxin Hao, Daniel Q. Naiman.
    p. cm.—(Quantitative applications in the social sciences; 149)
Includes bibliographical references and index.
ISBN 978-1-4129-2628-7 (pbk.)
    1. Social sciences—Statistical methods. 2. Regression analysis.
I. Naiman, Daniel Q. II. Title.
HA31.3.H36 2007
519.5′36—dc22

                                                                    2006035964

This book is printed on acid-free paper.

07   08   09   10   11   10   9   8   7   6   5   4   3   2   1

Acquisitions Editor:	Lisa Cuevas Shaw
Associate Editor:	Sean Connelly
Editorial Assistant:	Karen Greene
Production Editor:	Melanie Birdsall
Copy Editor:	Kevin Beck
Typesetter:	C&M Digitals (P) Ltd.
Proofreader:	Cheryl Rivard
Indexer:	Sheila Bodell
Cover Designer:	Candice Harman
Marketing Manager:	Stephanie Adams

CONTENTS

SERIES EDITOR'S INTRODUCTION

The classical linear-regression model has been part and parcel of a quantitative social scientist's methodology for at least four decades. The Quantitative Applications in the Social Sciences series has covered the topic well, with at least the following numbers focused centrally on the classical linear regression: Nos. 22, 29, 50, 57, 79, 92, and 93. There are many more treatments in the series of various extensions of the linear regression, such as logit, probit, event history, generalized linear, and generalized non-parametric models as well as linear-regression models of censored, sample-selected, truncated, and missing data, as well as many other related methods, including analysis of variance, analysis of covariance, causal modeling, log-linear modeling, multiple comparisons, and time-series analysis.

The central aim of the classical regression is to estimate the means of a response variable conditional on the values of the explanatory variables. This works well when regression assumptions are met, but not when conditions are nonstandard. (For a thorough discussion of linear-regression assumptions, see No. 92, *Understanding Regression Assumptions,* by William Berry.) Two of them are the normality assumption and the homoscedasticity assumption. These two crucial assumptions may not be satisfied by some common social-science data. For example, (conditional) income distributions are seldom normal, and the dispersion of the annual compensations of chief executive officers tends to increase with firm size, an indication of heteroscedasticity. This is where quantile regression can help because it relaxes these assumptions. In addition, quantile regression offers the researcher a view—unobtainable through the classical regression—of the effect of explanatory variables on the (central and noncentral) location, scale, and shape of the distribution of the response variable.

The idea of quantile regression is not new, and in fact goes back to 1760, when the itinerant Croatian Jesuit Rudjer Josip Boscovich—a man who wore many hats including those of a physicist, an astronomer, a diplomat, a philosopher, a poet, and a mathematician—went to London for computational advice for his nascent method of median regression. However, the computational difficulty for such regression analysis posed a huge challenge until recent years. With today's fast computers and wide availability of statistical software packages such as R, SAS, and Stata that implement the quantile-regression procedure, fitting a quantile-regression model to data has become easy. However, we have so far had no introduction in the series to the method to explain what quantile regression is all about.

Hao and Naiman's *Quantile Regression* is a truly welcome addition to the series. They present the concept of quantiles and quantile functions, specify the quantile-regression model, discuss its estimation and inference, and demonstrate the interpretation of quantile-regression estimates—transformed and not—with clear examples. They also provide a complete example of applying quantile regression to the analysis of income inequality in the United States in 1991 and 2001, to help fix the ideas and procedures. This book, then, fills a gap in the series and will help make quantile regression more accessible to many social scientists.

—*Tim F. Liao*
Series Editor

ACKNOWLEDGMENTS

Lingxin first became interested in using quantile regression to study race, immigration, and wealth stratification after learning of Buchinsky's work (1994), which applied quantile regression to wage inequality. This interest led to frequent discussions about methodological and mathematical issues related to quantile regression with Dan, who had first learned about the subject as a graduate student under Steve Portnoy at the University of Illinois. In the course of our conversations, we agreed that an empirically oriented introduction to quantile regression would be vital to the social-science research community. Particularly, it would provide easier access to necessary tools for social scientists who seek to uncover the impact of social factors on not only the mean but also the shape of a response distribution.

We gratefully acknowledge our colleagues in the Departments of Sociology and Applied Mathematics and Statistics at The Johns Hopkins University for their enthusiastic encouragement and support. In addition, we are grateful for the aid that we received from the Acheson J. Duncan Fund for the Advancement of Research in Statistics. Our gratitude further extends to additional support from the attendees of seminars at various universities and from the Sage QASS editor, Dr. Tim F. Liao. Upon the completion of the book, we wish to acknowledge the excellent research and editorial assistance from Xue Mary Lin, Sahan Savas Karatasli, Julie J. H. Kim, and Caitlin Cross-Barnet. The two anonymous reviewers of the manuscript also provided us with extremely helpful comments and beneficial suggestions, which led to a much-improved version of this book. Finally, we dedicate this book to our respective parents, who continue to inspire us.

QUANTILE REGRESSION

Lingxin Hao
The Johns Hopkins University

Daniel Q. Naiman
The Johns Hopkins University

1. INTRODUCTION

The purpose of regression analysis is to expose the relationship between a response variable and predictor variables. In real applications, the response variable cannot be predicted exactly from the predictor variables. Instead, the response for a fixed value of each predictor variable is a random variable. For this reason, we often summarize the behavior of the response for fixed values of the predictors using measures of central tendency. Typical measures of central tendency are the average value (mean), the middle value (median), or the most likely value (mode).

Traditional regression analysis is focused on the mean; that is, we summarize the relationship between the response variable and predictor variables by describing the mean of the response for each fixed value of the predictors, using a function we refer to as the *conditional mean* of the response. The idea of modeling and fitting the *conditional-mean function* is at the core of a broad family of regression-modeling approaches, including the familiar simple linear-regression model, multiple regression, models with heteroscedastic errors using weighted least squares, and nonlinear-regression models.

Conditional-mean models have certain attractive properties. Under ideal conditions, they are capable of providing a complete and parsimonious description of the relationship between the covariates and the response distribution. In addition, using conditional-mean models leads to estimators (least squares and maximum likelihood) that possess attractive statistical properties, are easy to calculate, and are straightforward to interpret. Such models have been generalized in various ways to allow for heteroscedastic errors so that given the predictors, modeling of the conditional mean and conditional scale of the response can be carried out simultaneously.

Conditional-mean modeling has been applied widely in the social sciences, particularly in the past half century, and regression modeling of the relationship between a continuous response and covariates via least squares and its generalization is now seen as an essential tool. More recently, models for binary response data, such as logistic and probit models and Poisson regression models for count data, have become increasingly popular in social-science research. These approaches fit naturally within the conditional-mean modeling framework. While quantitative social-science researchers have applied advanced methods to relax some basic modeling assumptions under the conditional-mean framework, this framework itself is seldom questioned.

The conditional-mean framework has inherent limitations. First, when summarizing the response for fixed values of predictor variables, the conditional-mean model cannot be readily extended to noncentral locations, which is precisely where the interests of social-science research often reside. For instance, studies of economic inequality and mobility have intrinsic interest in the poor (lower tail) and the rich (upper tail). Educational researchers seek to understand and reduce group gaps at preestablished achievement levels (e.g., the three criterion-referenced levels: basic, proficient, and advanced). Thus, the focus on the central location has long distracted researchers from using appropriate and relevant techniques to address research questions regarding noncentral locations on the response distribution. Using conditional-mean models to address these questions may be inefficient or even miss the point of the research altogether.

Second, the model assumptions are not always met in the real world. In particular, the homoscedasticity assumption frequently fails, and focusing exclusively on central tendencies can fail to capture informative trends in the response distribution. Also, heavy-tailed distributions commonly occur in social phenomena, leading to a preponderance of outliers. The conditional mean can then become an inappropriate and misleading measure of central location because it is heavily influenced by outliers.

Third, the focal point of central location has long steered researchers' attention away from the properties of the whole distribution. It is quite natural to go beyond location and scale effects of predictor variables on the response and ask how changes in the predictor variables affect the underlying *shape* of the distribution of the response. For example, much social-science research focuses on social stratification and inequality, areas that require close examination of the properties of a distribution. The central location, the scale, the skewness, and other higher-order properties—not central location alone—characterize a distribution. Thus, conditional-mean models are inherently ill equipped to characterize the relationship between a response distribution and predictor variables. Examples of inequality topics include economic inequality in wages, income, and wealth; educational inequality in academic achievement; health inequality in height, weight, incidence of disease, drug addiction, treatment, and life expectancy; and inequality in well-being induced by social policies. These topics have often been studied under the conditional-mean framework, while other, more relevant distributional properties have been ignored.

An alternative to conditional-mean modeling has roots that can be traced to the mid-18th century. This approach can be referred to as conditional-median modeling, or simply median regression. It addresses some of the issues mentioned above regarding the choice of a measure of central tendency. The method replaces least-squares estimation with least-absolute-distance estimation. While the least-squares method is simple to implement without high-powered computing capabilities, least-absolute-distance estimation demands significantly greater computing power. It was not until the late 1970s, when computing technology was combined with algorithmic developments such as linear programming, that median-regression modeling via least-absolute-distance estimation became practical.

The median-regression model can be used to achieve the same goal as conditional-mean-regression modeling: to represent the relationship between the central location of the response and a set of covariates. However, when the distribution is highly skewed, the mean can be challenging to interpret while the median remains highly informative. As a consequence, conditional-median modeling has the potential to be more useful.

The median is a special *quantile,* one that describes the central location of a distribution. Conditional-median regression is a special case of quantile regression in which the conditional .5th quantile is modeled as a function of covariates. More generally, other quantiles can be used to describe noncentral positions of a distribution. The *quantile* notion generalizes specific terms like *quartile, quintile, decile,* and *percentile.* The pth quantile denotes that value of the response below which the proportion of the population is p. Thus, quantiles can specify any position of a distribution. For example, 2.5% of the population lies below the .025th quantile.

Koenker and Bassett (1978) introduced *quantile regression,* which models conditional quantiles as functions of predictors. The quantile-regression model is a natural extension of the linear-regression model. While the linear-regression model specifies the change in the conditional mean of the dependent variable associated with a change in the covariates, the quantile-regression model specifies changes in the conditional quantile. Since any quantile can be used, it is possible to model any predetermined position of the distribution. Thus, researchers can choose positions that are tailored to their specific inquiries. Poverty studies concern the low-income population; for example, the bottom 11.3% of the population lived in poverty in 2000 (U.S. Census Bureau, 2001). Tax-policy studies concern the rich, for example, the top 4% of the population (Shapiro & Friedman, 2001). Conditional-quantile models offer the flexibility to focus on these population segments whereas conditional-mean models do not.

Since multiple quantiles can be modeled, it is possible to achieve a more complete understanding of how the response distribution is affected by predictors, including information about shape change. A set of equally spaced conditional quantiles (e.g., every 5% or 1% of the population) can characterize the shape of the conditional distribution in addition to its central location. The ability to model shape change provides a significant methodological leap forward in social research on inequality. Traditionally, inequality studies are non-model based; approaches include the Lorenz curve, the Gini coefficient, Theil's measure of entropy, the coefficient of variation, and the standard deviation of the log-transformed distribution. In another book for the Sage QASS series, we will develop conditional Lorenz and Gini coefficients, as well as other inequality measures based on quantile-regression models.

Quantile-regression models can be easily fit by minimizing a generalized measure of distance using algorithms based on linear programming. As a result, quantile regression is now a practical tool for researchers. Software packages familiar to social scientists offer readily accessed commands for fitting quantile-regression models.

A decade and a half after Koenker and Bassett first introduced quantile regression, empirical applications of quantile regression started to grow rapidly. Empirical researchers took advantage of quantile regression's ability to examine the impact of predictor variables on the response distribution. Two of the earliest empirical papers by economists (Buchinsky, 1994; Chamberlain, 1994) provided practical examples of how to apply quantile regression to the study of wages. Quantile regression allowed them to examine the entire conditional distribution of wages and determine if the returns to schooling, and experience and the effects of union membership differed across wage quantiles. The use of quantile regression to analyze wages increased and expanded to address additional topics such as changes in wage distribution (Machado & Mata, 2005; Melly,

2005), wage distributions within specific industries (Budd & McCall, 2001), wage gaps between whites and minorities (Chay & Honore, 1998) and between men and women (Fortin & Lemieux, 1998), educational attainment and wage inequality (Lemieux, 2006), and the intergenerational transfer of earnings (Eide & Showalter, 1999). The use of quantile regression also expanded to address the quality of schooling (Bedi & Edwards, 2002; Eide, Showalter, & Sims, 2002) and demographics' impact on infant birth weight (Abreveya, 2001). Quantile regression also spread to other fields, notably sociology (Hao, 2005, 2006a, 2006b), ecology and environmental sciences (Cade, Terrell, & Schroeder, 1999; Scharf, Juanes, & Sutherland, 1989), and medicine and public health (Austin et al., 2005; Wei et al., 2006).

This book aims to introduce the quantile-regression model to a broad audience of social scientists who are interested in modeling both the location and shape of the distribution they wish to study. It is also written for readers who are concerned about the sensitivity of linear-regression models to skewed distributions and outliers. The book builds on the basic literature of Koenker and his colleagues (e.g., Koenker, 1994; Koenker, 2005; Koenker & Bassett, 1978; Koenker & d'Orey, 1987; Koenker & Hallock, 2001; Koenker & Machado, 1999) and makes two further contributions. We develop conditional-quantile-based shape-shift measures based on quantile-regression estimates. These measures provide direct answers to research questions about a covariate's impact on the shape of the response distribution. In addition, inequality research often uses log transformation of right-skewed responses to create a better model fit even though "inequality" in this case refers to raw-scale distributions. Therefore, we develop methods to obtain a covariate's effect on the location and shape of conditional-quantile functions in absolute terms from log-scale coefficients.

Drawn from our own research experience, this book is oriented toward those involved with empirical research. We take a didactic approach, using language and procedures familiar to social scientists. These include clearly defined terms, simplified equations, illustrative graphs, tables and graphs based on empirical data, and computational codes using statistical software popular among social scientists. Throughout the book, we draw examples from our own research on household income distribution. In order to provide a gentle introduction to quantile regression, we use simplified model specifications wherein the conditional-quantile functions for the raw or log responses are linear and additive in the covariates. As in linear regression, the methodology we present is easily adapted to more complex model specifications, including, for example, interaction terms and polynomial or spline functions of covariates.

Quantile-regression modeling provides a natural complement to modeling approaches dealt with extensively in the QASS series: *Understanding Regression Assumptions* (Berry, 1993), *Understanding Regression Analysis* (Schroeder, 1986), and *Multiple Regression in Practice* (Berry & Feldman, 1985). Other books in the series can be used as references to some of the techniques discussed in this book, e.g., *Bootstrapping* (Mooney, 1993) and *Linear Programming* (Feiring, 1986).

The book is organized as follows. Chapter 2 defines quantiles and quantile functions in two ways—using the cumulative distribution function and solving a minimization problem. It also develops quantile-based measures of location and shape of a distribution in comparison with distributional moments (e.g., mean, standard deviation). Chapter 3 introduces the basics of the quantile-regression model (QRM) in comparison with the linearregression model, including the model setup, the estimator, and properties. The numerous quantile-regression equations with quantile-specific parameters are a unique feature of the quantile-regression model. We describe how quantile-regression fits are obtained by making use of the minimum distance principle. The QRM possesses properties such as monotonic equivariance and robustness to distributional assumptions, which produce flexible, nonsensitive estimates, properties that are absent in the linear-regression model. Chapter 4 discusses inferences for the quantile-regression model. In addition to introducing the asymptotic inference for quantile-regression coefficients, the chapter emphasizes the utility and feasibility of the bootstrap method. In addition, this chapter briefly discusses goodness of fit for quantile-regression models, analogous to that for linear-regression models. Chapter 5 develops various ways to interpret estimates from the quantile-regression model. Going beyond the traditional examination of the effect of a covariate on specific conditional quantiles, such as the median or off-central quantiles, Chapter 5 focuses on a distributional interpretation. It illustrates graphical interpretations of quantile-regression estimates and quantitative measures of shape changes from quantile-regression estimates, including location shifts, scale shifts, and skewness shifts. Chapter 6 considers issues related to monotonically transformed response variables. We develop two ways to obtain a covariate's effect on the location and shape of conditional-quantile functions in absolute terms from log-scale coefficients. Chapter 7 presents a systematic application of the techniques introduced and developed in the book. This chapter analyzes the sources of the persistent and widening income inequality in the United States between 1991 and 2001. Finally, the Appendix provides Stata codes for performing the analytic tasks described in Chapter 7.

2. QUANTILES AND QUANTILE FUNCTIONS

Describing and comparing the distributional attributes of populations is essential to social science. The simplest and most familiar measures used to describe a distribution are the mean for the central location and the standard deviation for the dispersion. However, restricting attention to the mean and standard deviation alone leads us to ignore other important properties that offer more insight into the distribution. For many researchers, attributes of interest often have skewed distributions, for which the mean and standard deviation are not necessarily the best measures of location and shape. To characterize the location and shape of asymmetric distributions, this chapter introduces quantiles, quantile functions, and their properties by way of the cumulative distribution function (cdf). It also develops quantile-based measures of location and shape of a distribution and, finally, redefines a quantile as a solution to a certain minimization problem.

CDFs, Quantiles, and Quantile Functions

To describe the distribution of a random variable Y, we can use its cumulative distribution function (cdf). The cdf is the function F_Y that gives, for each value of y, the proportion of the population for which $Y \leq y$. Figure 2.1 shows the cdf for the standard normal distribution. The cdf can be used to calculate the proportion of the population for any range of values of y. We see in Figure 2.1 that $F_Y(0) = .5$ and $F_Y(1.28) = .9$. The cdf can be used to calculate all other probabilities involving Y. In particular: $P[Y > y] = 1 - F_y(y)$ (e.g., in Figure 2.1, $P[Y > 1.28] = 1 - F_y(1.28) = 1 - 0.9 = 0.1$) and $P[a < Y \leq b] = F_Y(b) - F_Y(a)$ (e.g., in Figure 2.1, $P[0 \leq Y \leq 1.28] = F_Y(1.28) - F_Y(0) = 0.40$)). The two most important properties of a cdf are monotonicity (i.e., $F(y_1) \leq F(y_2)$ whenever $y_1 \leq y_2$) and its behavior at infinity $\lim_{y \to -\infty} F(y) = 0$ and $\lim_{y \to +\infty} F(y) = 1$. For a continuous random variable Y, we can also represent its distribution using a probability density function f_y defined as the function with the property that $P[a \leq Y \leq b] = \int_{y=a}^{b} f_Y dy$ for all choices of a and b.

Returning to the issue of the inadequacy of location and spread for fully describing a distribution, suppose we are told that the mean household income for whites (W) exceeds that of blacks (B) by \$20,500. This could be described simply by a shift in the location of the distribution while retaining the shape (see the corresponding density functions in Figure 2.2a), so that the relationship between the distributions is expressed by $F^B(y) = F^W(y - 20{,}500)$. The difference in distributions may consist of a change in both location and scale (see the corresponding density functions in Figure 2.2b), so that the relationship between the distributions takes the general form $F^B(y) = F^W(ay - c)$ for constants a and c ($a > 0$). This is the

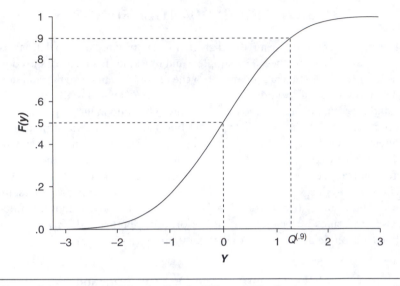

Figure 2.1   The CDF for the Standard Normal Distribution

case when both the mean and the variance of y differ between populations W and B. Knowledge of measures of location and scale, for example, the mean and standard deviation, or alternatively the median and interquartile range, enables us to compare the attribute Y between the two distributions.

As distributions become less symmetrical, more complex summary measures are needed. Consideration of quantiles and quantile functions leads to a rich collection of summary measures. Continuing the discussion of a cdf, F, for some population attribute, the pth quantile of this distribution, denoted by $Q^{(p)}(F)$ (or simply $Q^{(p)}$ when it is clear what distribution is being discussed), is the value of the inverse of the cdf at p, that is, a value of y such that $F(y) = p$. Thus, the proportion of the population with an attribute below $Q^{(p)}$ is p. For example, in the standard normal case (see Figure 2.1), $F(1.28) = .9$, so $Q^{(.9)} = 1.28$, that is, the proportion of the population with the attribute below 1.28 is .9 or 90%.

Analogous to the population cdf, we consider the *empirical* or *sample* cdf associated with a sample. For a sample consisting of values $y_1, y_2, \ldots, y_n$, the empirical cdf gives the proportion of the sample values that is less than or equal to any given y. More formally, the empirical cdf $\hat{F}$ is defined by

$\hat{F}(y) =$ the proportion of sample values less than or equal to y.

As an example, consider a sample consisting of 20 households with incomes of $3,000, $3,500, $4,000, $4,300, $4,600, $5,000, $5,000, $5,000, $8,000, $9,000, $10,000, $11,000, $12,000, $15,000, $17,000, $20,000,

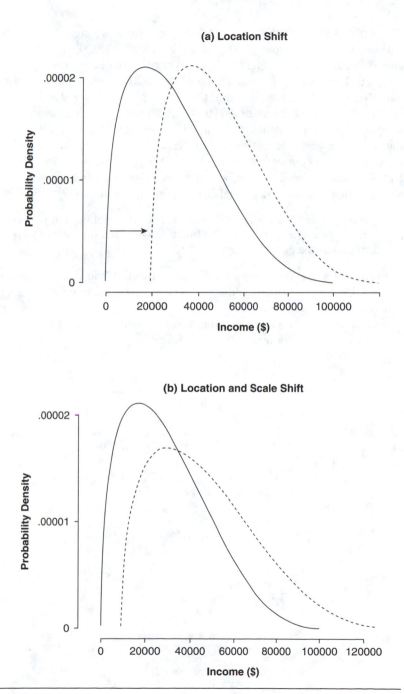

Figure 2.2   Location Shift and Location and Scale Shift: Hypothetical Data

$32,000, $38,000, $56,000, and $84,000. Since there are eight households with incomes at or below $5,000, we have $F(5,000) = 8/20$. A plot of the empirical cdf is shown in Figure 2.3, which consists of one jump and several flat parts. For example, there is a jump of size 3/20 at 5,000, indicating that the value of 5,000 appears three times in the sample. There are also flat parts such as the portion between 56,000 and 84,000, indicating that there are no sample values in the interior of this interval. Since the empirical cdf can be flat, there are values having multiple inverses. For example, in Figure 2.3 there appears to be a continuum of choices for $Q^{(.975)}$ between 56,000 and 84,000. Thus, we need to exercise some care when we introduce quantiles and quantile functions for a general distribution with the following definition:

Definition. The pth quantile $Q^{(p)}$ of a cdf F is the minimum of the set of values y such that $F(y) \geq p$. The function $Q^{(p)}$ (as a function of p) is referred to as the quantile function of F.

Figure 2.4 shows an example of a quantile function and the corresponding cdf. Observe that the quantile function is a monotonic nondecreasing function that is continuous from below.

As a special case we can talk about *sample quantiles,* which can be used to estimate quantiles of a sampled distribution.

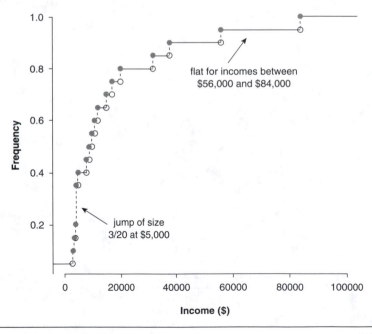

Figure 2.3   CDF With Jumps and Flat Parts

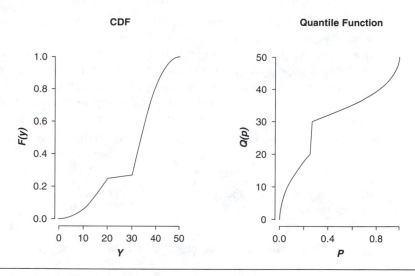

CDF

Quantile Function

Figure 2.4   CDF and Corresponding Quantile Function

Definition. Given a sample $y_1, \ldots, y_n$, we define its *p*th sample quantile $\hat{Q}^{(p)}$ to be the *p*th quantile of the corresponding empirical cdf $\hat{F}$, that is, $\hat{Q}^{(P)} = Q^{(p)}(\hat{F})$. The corresponding quantile function is referred to as the sample quantile function.

Sample quantiles are closely related to *order statistics*. Given a sample $y_1, \ldots, y_n$, we can rank the data values from smallest to largest and rewrite the sample as $y_{(1)}, \ldots, y_{(n)}$, where $y_{(1)} \le y_{(2)} \le \ldots \le y_{(n)}$. Data values are repeated if they appear multiple times. We refer to $y_{(i)}$ as the *i*th-order statistic corresponding to the sample. The connection between order statistics and sample quantiles is simple to describe: For a sample of size *n*, the (*k/n*)th sample quantile is given by $y_{(k)}$. For example, in the sample of 20 data points given above, the (4/20)th sample quantile, that is, the 20th percentile, is given by $\hat{Q}^{(.2)} = y_{(4)} = 4,300$.

Sampling Distribution of a Sample Quantile

It is important to note how sample quantiles behave in large samples. For a large sample $y_1, \ldots, y_n$ drawn from a distribution with quantile function $Q^{(p)}$ and probability density function $f = F'$, the distribution of $\hat{Q}^{(p)}$ is approximately normal with mean $Q^{(p)}$ and variance $\dfrac{p(1-p)}{n} \cdot \dfrac{1}{f(Q^{(p)})^2}$. In particular, this variance of the sample distribution is completely determined by the probability density evaluated *at the quantile*. The dependence on the density at the quantile has a simple intuitive explanation: If there are more data nearby (higher density),

12

the sample quantile is less variable; conversely, if there are fewer data nearby (low density), the sample quantile is more variable.

To estimate the quantile sampling variability, we make use of the variance approximation above, which requires a way of estimating the unknown probability density function. A standard approach to this estimation is illustrated in Figure 2.5, where the slope of the tangent line to the function $Q^{(p)}$ at the point p is the derivative of the quantile function with respect to p, or equivalently, the inverse density function: $\frac{d}{dp}Q^{(p)} = 1/f(Q^{(p)})$. This term can be approximated by the difference quotient $\frac{1}{2h}(\hat{Q}^{(p+h)} - \hat{Q}^{(p-h)})$, which is the slope of the secant line through the points $(p-h, \hat{Q}^{(p-h)})$ and $(p+h, \hat{Q}^{(p+h)})$ for some small value of h.

Quantile-Based Measures of Location and Shape

Social scientists are familiar with the quantile-based measure of central location; namely, instead of the mean (the first moment of a density function), the median (i.e., the .5th quantile) has been used to indicate the

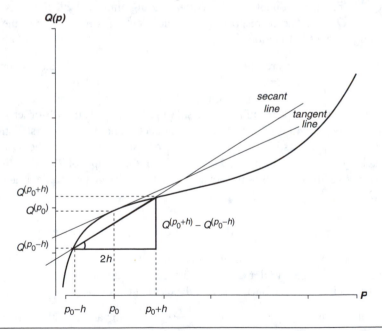

Figure 2.5   Illustrating How to Estimate the Slope of a Quantile Function

NOTE: The derivative of the function $Q^{(p)}$ at the point p_0 (the slope of the tangent line) is approximated by the slope of the secant line, which is $(Q^{(p_0+h)} - Q^{(p_0-h)})/2h$.

center of a skewed distribution. Using quantile-based location allows one to investigate more general notions of location beyond just the center of a distribution. Specifically, we can examine a location at the lower tail (e.g., the .1th quantile) or a location at the upper tail (e.g., the .9th quantile) for research questions regarding specific subpopulations.

Two basic properties describe the shape of a distribution: scale and skewness. Traditionally, scale is measured by the standard deviation, which is based on the second moment of a distribution involving a quadratic function of the deviations of data points from the mean. This measure is easy to interpret for a symmetric distribution, but when the distribution becomes highly asymmetric, its interpretation tends to break down. It is also misleading for heavy-tailed distributions. Since many of the distributions used to describe social phenomena are skewed or heavy-tailed, using the standard deviation to characterize their scales becomes problematic. To capture the spread of a distribution without relying on the standard deviation, we measure spread using the following quantile-based scale measure (QSC) at a selected p:

$$QSC^{(p)} = Q^{(1-p)} - Q^{(p)} \text{ for } p < .5. \qquad [2.1]$$

We can obtain the spread for the middle 95% of the population between $Q^{(.025)}$ and $Q^{(.975)}$, or the middle 50% of the population between $Q^{(.25)}$ and $Q^{(.75)}$ (the conventional interquartile range), or the spread of any desirable middle $100(1 - 2p)\%$ of the population.

The QSC measure not only offers a direct and straightforward measure of scale but also facilitates the development of a rich class of model-based scale-shift measures (developed in Chapter 5). In contrast, a model-based approach that separates out a predictor's effect in terms of a change in scale as measured by the standard deviation limits the possible patterns that could be discovered.

A second measure of a distributional shape is skewness. This property is the focus of much inequality research. Skewness is measured using a cubic function of data points' deviations from the mean. When the data are symmetrically distributed about the sample mean, the value of skewness is zero. A negative value indicates left skewness and a positive value indicates right skewness. Skewness can be interpreted as saying that there is an imbalance between the spread below and above the median.

Although skewness has long been used to describe the nonnormality of a distribution, the fact that it is based on higher moments of the distribution is confining. We seek more flexible methods for linking properties like skewness to covariates. In contrast to moment-based measures, sample quantiles can be used to describe the nonnormality of a distribution in a host of ways. The simple connection between quantiles and the shape of a distribution enables further development of methods for modeling shape changes (this method is developed in Chapter 5).

Uneven upper and lower spreads can be expressed using the quantile function. Figure 2.6 describes two quantile functions for a normal distribution and a right-skewed distribution. The quantile function for the normal distribution is symmetric around the .5th quantile (the median). For example, Figure 2.6a shows that the slope of the quantile function at the .1th quantile is the same as the slope at the .9th quantile. This is true for all other corresponding lower and upper quantiles. By contrast, the quantile function for a skewed distribution is asymmetric around the median. For instance, Figure 2.6b shows that the slope of the quantile function at the .1th quantile is very different from the slope at the .9th quantile.

Let the *upper spread* refer to the spread above the median and the *lower spread* refer to the spread below the median. The upper spread and the lower spread are equal for a symmetric distribution. On the other hand, the lower spread is much shorter than the upper spread in a right-skewed distribution. We quantify the measure of quantile-based skewness (QSK) as a ratio of the upper spread to the lower spread minus one:

$$QSK^{(p)} = (Q^{(1-p)} - Q^{(.5)})/(Q^{(.5)} - Q^{(p)}) - 1 \text{ for } p < 0.5. \qquad [2.2]$$

The quantity $QSK^{(p)}$ is recentered using subtraction of one, so that it takes the value zero for a symmetric distribution. A value greater than zero indicates right-skewness and a value less than 0 indicates left-skewness.

Table 2.1 shows 9 quantiles of the symmetric and right-skewed distribution in Figure 2.6b, their upper and lower spreads, and the $QSK^{(p)}$ at four different values of p. The $QSK^{(p)}$s are 0 for the symmetric example, while they range from 0.3 to 1.1 for the right-skewed distribution. This definition of $QSK^{(p)}$ is simple and straightforward and has the potential to be extended to measure the skewness shift caused by a covariate (see Chapter 5).

So far we have defined quantiles in terms of the cdf and have developed quantile-based shape measures. Readers interested in an alternative definition of quantiles that will facilitate the understanding of the quantile-regression estimator (in the next chapter) are advised to continue on to the next section. Others may wish to skip to the Summary Section.

Quantile as a Solution to a Certain Minimization Problem

A quantile can also be considered as a solution to a certain minimization problem. We introduce this redefinition because of its implication for the quantile-regression estimator to be discussed in the next chapter. We start with the median, the .5th quantile.

To motivate the minimization problem, we first consider the familiar mean, μ, of the y distribution. We can measure how far a given data point of Y is from the value μ using the squared deviation $(Y - \mu)^2$, and then how far Y is from μ,

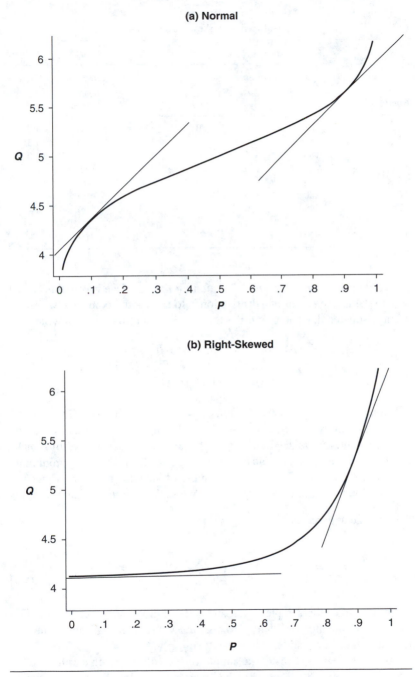

(a) Normal

(b) Right-Skewed

Figure 2.6   Normal Versus Skewed Quantile Functions

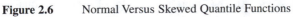

TABLE 2.1
Quantile-Based Skewness Measure

Proportion of Population	Symmetric			Right-Skewed		
	Quantile	Lower or Upper Spread	QSK	Quantile	Lower or Upper Spread	QSK
0.1	100	110	0	130	60	1.7
0.2	150	60	0	150	40	1.3
0.3	180	30	0	165	25	1.0
0.4	200	10	0	175	15	0.3
0.5	210	—	—	190	—	—
0.6	220	10	—	210	20	—
0.7	240	30	—	240	50	—
0.8	270	60	—	280	90	—
0.9	320	110	—	350	160	—

on average, by the *mean squared deviation* $E[(Y - \mu)^2]$. One way to think about how to define the *center* of a distribution is to ask for the point μ at which the average squared deviation from Y is minimized. Therefore, we can write

$$E[(Y - \mu)^2] = E[Y^2] - 2E[Y]\mu + \mu^2$$
$$= (\mu - E[Y])^2 + (E[Y^2] - (E[Y])^2).$$
$$= (\mu - E[Y])^2 + Var(Y) \qquad [2.3]$$

Because the second term $Var(Y)$ is constant, we minimize Equation 2.3 by minimizing the first term $(\mu - E[Y])^2$. Taking $\mu = E[Y]$ makes the first term zero and minimizes Equation 2.3 because any other values of μ make the first term positive and cause Equation 2.3 to depart from the minimum.

Similarly, the sample mean for a sample of size n can also be viewed as the solution to a minimization problem. We seek the point μ that minimizes the average squared distance $\frac{1}{n}\sum_{i=1}^{n}(y_i - \mu)^2$:

$$\frac{1}{n}\sum_{i=1}^{n}(y_i - \mu)^2 = \frac{1}{n}\sum_{i=1}^{n}(\mu - \bar{y})^2 + \frac{1}{n}\sum_{i=1}^{n}(y_i - \bar{y})^2 = (\mu - \bar{y})^2 + s_y^2, \qquad [2.4]$$

where $\bar{y}$ denotes the sample mean, and s_y^2 the sample variance. The solution to this minimization problem is to take the value of μ that makes the first term as small as possible, that is, we take $\mu = \bar{y}$.

For concreteness, consider a sample of the following nine values: 0.23, 0.87, 1.36, 1.49, 1.89, 2.69, 3.10, 3.82, and 5.25. A plot of the mean squared distance of sample points from a given point μ is shown in Figure 2.7a. Note that the function to minimize is convex, with a smooth parabolic form.

The median m has a similar minimizing property. Instead of using squared distance, we can measure how far Y is from m by the absolute distance $|Y - m|$ and measure the average distance in the population from m by the *mean absolute distance* $E|Y - m|$. Again we can solve for the value m by minimizing $E|Y - m|$. As we shall see, the function of $|Y - m|$ is convex, so that the minimization solution is to find a point where the derivative with respect to m is zero or where the two *directional* derivatives disagree in sign. The solution is the median of the distribution. (A proof appears in the Appendix of this chapter.)

Similarly, we can work on the sample level. We define the mean absolute distance from m to the sample points by $\frac{1}{n}\sum_{i=1}^{n}|y_i - m|$. A plot of this function is given in Figure 2.7b for the same sample of nine points above. Compared with the function plotted in Figure 2.7a (the mean squared deviation), Figure 2.7b remains convex and parabolic in appearance. However, rather than being smooth, the function in Figure 2.7b is piecewise linear, with the slope changing precisely at each sample point. The minimum value of the function shown in this figure coincides with the median sample value of 1.89. This is a special case of a more general phenomenon. For any sample, the function defined by $f(m) = \frac{1}{n}\sum_{i=1}^{n}|y_i - m|$ is the sum of *V-shaped* functions $f_i(m) = |y_i - m|/n$ (see Figure 2.8 for the function f_i corresponding to the data point with $y_i = 1.49$). The function f_i takes a minimum value of zero when $m = y_i$ has a derivative of $-1/n$ for $m < y_i$ and $1/n$ for $m > y_i$. While the function is not differentiable at $m = y_i$, it does have a *directional* derivative there of $-1/n$ in the negative direction and $1/n$ in the positive direction. Being the sum of these functions, the directional derivative of f at m is $(r - s)/n$ in the negative direction and $(s - r)/n$ in the positive direction, where s is the number of data points to the right of m and r is the number of data points to the left of m. It follows that the minimum of f occurs when m has the same number of data points to its left and right, that is, when m is a sample median.

This representation of the median generalizes to the other quantiles as follows. For any $p \in (0,1)$, the distance from Y to a given q is measured by the absolute distance, but we apply a different weight depending on whether Y is to the left or to the right of q. Thus, we define the distance from Y to a given q as:

$$d_p(Y, q) = \begin{cases} (1 - p)|Y - q| & Y < q \\ p|Y - q| & Y \geq q \end{cases}. \qquad [2.5]$$

We look for the value q that minimizes the mean distance from Y: $E[d_p(Y,q)]$. The minimum occurs when q is the pth quantile (see Appendix

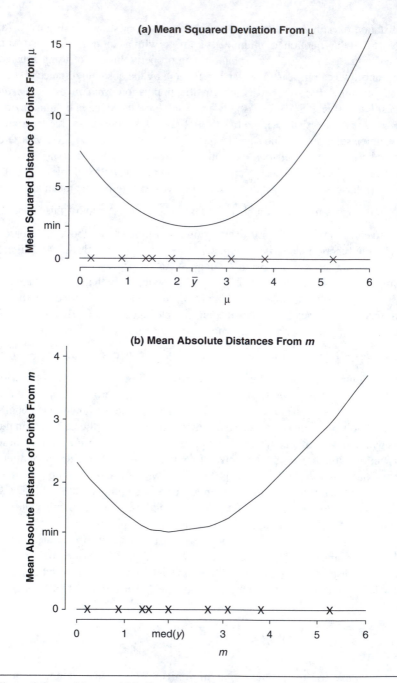

Figure 2.7   Mean and Median as Solutions to a Minimization Problem

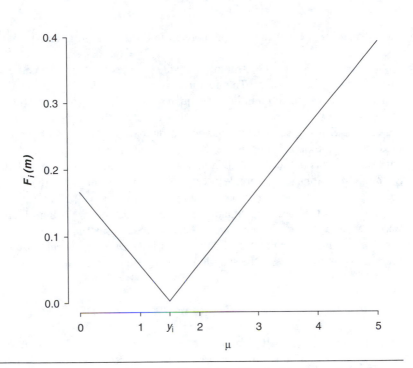

Figure 2.8   *V-Shaped* Function Used to Describe the Median as the Solution to a Minimization Problem

of this chapter). Similarly, the *p*th sample quantile is the value of *q* that minimizes the average (weighted) distance:

$$\frac{1}{n}\sum_{i=1}^{n} d_p(y_i, q) = \frac{1-p}{n}\sum_{y_i < q}|y_i - q| + \frac{p}{n}\sum_{y_i > q}|y_i - q|.$$

Properties of Quantiles

One basic property of quantiles is *monotone equivariance* property. It states that if we apply a monotone transformation *h* (for example, the exponential or logarithmic function) to a random variable, the quantiles are obtained by applying the same transformation to the quantile function. In other words, if *q* is the *p*th quantile of *Y*, then *h*(*q*) is the *p*th quantile of *h*(*Y*). An analogous statement can be made for sample quantiles. For example, for the sample data, since we know that the 20th percentile is 4,300, if we make a log transformation of the data, the 20th percentile for the resulting data will be log (4,300) = 8.37.

Another basic property of sample quantiles relates to their insensitivity to the influence of outliers. This feature, which has an analog in quantile regression, helps make quantiles and quantile-based procedures useful in many contexts. Given a sample of data $x_1, \ldots, x_n$ with sample median m, we can modify the sample by changing a data value x_i that is above the median to some other value above the median. Similarly, we can change a data value that is below the median to some other value below the median. Such modifications to the sample have no effect on the sample median.[1] An analogous property holds for the pth sample quantile as well.

We contrast this with the situation for the sample mean: Changing any sample value x_i to some other value $x_i + \Delta$ changes the sample mean by Δ/n. Thus, the influence of individual data points is *bounded* for sample quantiles and is *unbounded* for the sample mean.

Summary

This chapter introduces the notions of quantile and quantile function. We define quantiles and quantile functions by way of the cumulative distribution function. We develop quantile-based measures of location and shape of a distribution and highlight their utility by comparing them with conventional distribution moments. We also redefine quantiles as a solution to a minimization problem, preparing the reader for a better understanding of the quantile regression estimator. With these preparations, we proceed to the next chapter on the quantile-regression model and its estimator.

Note

1. To be precise, this assumes that the sample size is odd. If the sample size is even, then the sample median is defined as the average of the $(n/2)$th and $(n/2 + 1)$th order statistics, and the statement holds if we modify a data value above (or below) the $(n/2 + 1)$th (or $(n/2)$th) order statistic, keeping it above (or below) that value.

Chapter 2 Appendix

A Proof: Median and Quantiles as
Solutions to a Minimization Problem

To make things simple, we assume that the cdf F has a probability density function f. To see why median can be defined as a minimization problem, we can write

$$
\begin{aligned}
E|Y - m| &= \int_{-\infty}^{+\infty} |y - m| f(y) dy \\
&= \int_{y=-\infty}^{m} |y - m| f(y) dy + \int_{y=m}^{+\infty} |y - m| f(y) dy \\
&= \int_{y=-\infty}^{m} (m - y) f(y) dy + \int_{y=m}^{+\infty} (y - m) f(y) dy.
\end{aligned}
$$

$$[A.1]$$

As Figure 2.7b shows, Equation A.1 is a convex function. Differentiating with respect to m and setting the partial derivative to zero will lead to the solution for the minimum. The partial derivative of the first term is:

$$
\frac{\partial}{\partial m} \int_{y=-\infty}^{m} (m - y) f(y) dy = (m - y) f(y)|_{y=m} + \int_{y=-\infty}^{m} \frac{\partial}{\partial m} (m - y) f(y) dy
$$

$$
= \int_{y=-\infty}^{m} f(y) dy = F(m)
$$

and the partial derivative of the second term is:

$$
\frac{\partial}{\partial m} \int_{y=m}^{+\infty} (y - m) f(y) dy = - \int_{y=m}^{+\infty} f(y) dy = -(1 - F(m)).
$$

Combining these two partial derivatives leads to:

$$\frac{\partial}{\partial m}\int_{-\infty}^{+\infty}|y-m|f(y)dy = F(m) - (1 - F(m)) = 2F(m) - 1. \quad \text{[A.2]}$$

By setting $2F(m) - 1 = 0$, we solve for the value of $F(m) = 1/2$, that is, the median, to satisfy the minimization problem.

Repeating the above argument for quantiles, the partial derivative for quantiles corresponding to Equation A.2 is:

$$\frac{\partial}{\partial q}E[d_p(Y, q)] = (1 - p)F(q) - p(1 - F(q)) = F(q) - p. \quad \text{[A.3]}$$

We set the partial derivative $F(q) - p = 0$ and solve for the value of $F(q) = p$ that satisfies the minimization problem.

3. QUANTILE-REGRESSION MODEL AND ESTIMATION

The quantile functions described in Chapter 2 are adequate for describing and comparing univariate distributions. However, when we model the relationship between a response variable and a number of independent variables, it becomes necessary to introduce a regression-type model for the quantile function, the quantile-regression model (QRM). Given a set of covariates, the linear-regression model (LRM) specifies the *conditional-mean* function whereas the QRM specifies the *conditional-quantile* function. Using the LRM as a point of reference, this chapter introduces the QRM and its estimation. It makes comparisons between the basic model setup for the LRM and that for the QRM, a least-squares estimation for the LRM and an analogous estimation approach for the QRM, and the properties of the two types of models. We illustrate our basic points using empirical examples from analyses of household income.[1]

Linear-Regression Modeling and Its Shortcomings

The LRM is a standard statistical method widely used in social-science research, but it focuses on modeling the conditional mean of a response variable without accounting for the full conditional distributional properties of the response variable. In contrast, the QRM facilitates analysis of the full conditional distributional properties of the response variable. The QRM and LRM are similar in certain respects, as both models deal with a continuous response variable that is linear in unknown parameters, but the QRM and LRM model different quantities and rely on different assumptions about error terms. To better understand these similarities and differences, we lay out the LRM as a starting point, and then introduce the QRM. To aid the explication, we focus on the single covariate case. While extending to more than one covariate necessarily introduces additional complexity, the ideas remain essentially the same.

Let y be a continuous response variable depending on x. In our empirical example, the dependent variable is household income. For x, we use an interval variable, *ED* (the household head's years of schooling), or alternatively a dummy variable, *BLACK* (the head's race, 1 for black and 0 for white). We consider data consisting of pairs (x_i, y_i) for $i = 1, \ldots, n$ based on a sample of micro units (households in our example).

By LRM, we mean the standard linear-regression model

$$y_i = \beta_0 + \beta_1 x_i + \varepsilon_i,$$ [3.1]

where ε_i is identically, independently, and normally distributed with mean zero and unknown variance σ^2. As a consequence of the mean zero assumption, we see that the function $\beta_0 + \beta_1 x$ being fitted to the data corresponds to the conditional mean of y given x (denoted by $E[y|x]$), which is interpreted as the average in the population of y values corresponding to a fixed value of the covariate x.

For example, when we fit the linear-regression Equation 3.1 using years of schooling as the covariate, we obtain the prediction equation $\hat{y} = -23127 + 5633ED$, so that plugging in selected numbers of years of schooling leads to the following values of conditional means for income.

ED	9	12	16
$E(y \mid ED)$	$27,570	$44,469	$67,001

Assuming a perfect fit, we would interpret these values as the average income for people with a given number of years of schooling. For example, the average income for people with nine years of schooling is $27,570.

Analogously, when we take the covariate to be *BLACK*, the fitted regression equation takes the form $\hat{y} = 53466 - 18268BLACK$, and plugging in the values of this covariate yields the following values.

BLACK	0	1
$E(y \mid BLACK)$	$53,466	$35,198

Again assuming the fitted model to be a reflection of what happens at the population level, we would interpret these values as averages in subpopulations, for example, the average income is $53,466 for whites and $35,198 for blacks.

Thus, we see that a fundamental aspect of linear-regression models is that they attempt to describe how the location of the conditional distribution behaves by utilizing the mean of a distribution to represent its central tendency. Another key feature of the LRM is that it invokes a homoscedasticity assumption; that is, the conditional variance, $Var(y \mid x)$, is assumed to be a constant σ^2 for all values of the covariate. When homoscedasticity fails, it is possible to modify LRM by allowing for simultaneous modeling of the conditional mean and the conditional scale. For example, one can modify the model in Equation 3.1 to allow for modeling the conditional scale: $y_i = \beta_0 + \beta_1 x_i + e^\gamma \varepsilon_i$, where γ is an additional unknown parameter and we can write $Var(y \mid x) = \sigma^2 e^\gamma$.

Thus, utilizing LRM reveals important aspects of the relationship between covariates and a response variable, and can be adapted to perform the task of modeling what is arguably the most important form of shape change for a conditional distribution: scale change. However, the estimation of conditional scale is not always readily available in statistical software. In addition, linear-regression models impose significant constraints on the modeler, and it is challenging to use LRM to model more complex conditional shape shifts.

To illustrate the kind of shape shift that is difficult to model using LRM, imagine a somewhat extreme situation in which, for some population of interest, we have a response variable y and a covariate x with the property that the conditional distribution of y has the probability density of the form shown in Figure 3.1 for each given value of $x = 1, 2, 3$. The three probability density functions in this figure have the same mean and standard deviation. Since the conditional mean and scale for the response variable y do not vary with x, there is no information to be gleaned by fitting a linear-regression model to samples from these populations. In order to understand how the covariate affects the response variable, a new tool is required. Quantile regression is an appropriate tool for accomplishing this task.

A third distinctive feature of the LRM is its *normality assumption.* Because the LRM ensures that the ordinary least squares provide the best possible fit for the data, we use the LRM without making the normality assumption for purely descriptive purposes. However, in social-science research, the LRM is used primarily to test whether an explanatory variable

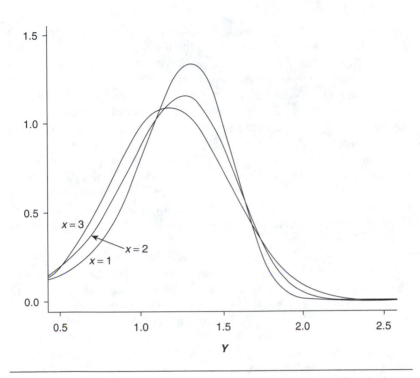

Figure 3.1   Conditional Distributions With the Same Mean and Standard
Deviation but Different Skewness

significantly affects the dependent variable. Hypothesis testing goes beyond
parameter estimation and requires determination of the sampling variability of estimators. Calculated p-values rely on the normality assumption or
on large-sample approximation. Violation of these conditions may cause
biases in p-values, thus leading to invalid hypothesis testing.

A related assumption made in the LRM is that the regression model used
is appropriate for all data, which we call the *one-model assumption.*
Outliers (cases that do not follow the relationship for the majority of the
data) in the LRM tend to have undue influence on the fitted regression line.
The usual practice used in the LRM is to identify outliers and eliminate
them. Both the notion of outliers and the practice of eliminating outliers
undermine much social-science research, particularly studies on social
stratification and inequality, as outliers and their relative positions to those
of the majority are important aspects of inquiry. In terms of modeling, one
would simultaneously need to model the relationship for the majority cases
and for the outlier cases, a task the LRM cannot accomplish.

All of the features just mentioned are exemplified in our household income data: the inadequacy of the conditional mean from a distributional point of view and violations of the homoscedasticity assumption, the normality assumption, and the one-model assumption. Figure 3.2 shows the distributions of income by education groups and racial groups. The location shifts among the three education groups and between blacks and whites are obvious, and their shape shifts are substantial. Therefore, the conditional mean from the LRM fails to capture the shape shifts caused by changes in the covariate (education or race). In addition, since the spreads differ substantially among the education groups and between the two racial groups, the homoscedasticity assumption is violated, and the standard errors are not estimated precisely. All box graphs in Figure 3.2 are right-skewed. Conditional-mean and conditional-scale models are not able to detect these kinds of shape changes.

By examining residual plots, we have identified seven outliers, including three cases with 18 years of schooling having an income of more than $505,215 and four cases with 20 years of schooling having an income of more than $471,572. When we add a dummy variable indicating membership in this outlier class to the regression model of income on education, we find that these cases contribute an additional $483,544 to the intercept.

These results show that the LRM approach can be inadequate for a variety of reasons, including heteroscedasticity and outlier assumptions and the failure to detect multiple forms of shape shifts. These inadequacies are not restricted to the study of household income but also appear when other measures are considered. Therefore, it is desirable to have an alternative approach that is built to handle heteroscedasticity and outliers and detect various forms of shape changes.

As pointed out above, the conditional mean fails to identify shape shifts. The conditional-mean models also do not always correctly model central location shifts if the response distribution is asymmetric. For a symmetric distribution, the mean and median coincide, but the mean of a skewed distribution is no longer the same as the median (the .5th quantile). Table 3.1 shows a set of brief statistics describing the household income distribution. The right-skewness of the distribution makes the mean considerably larger than the median for both the total sample and for education and racial groups (see the first two rows of Table 3.1). When the mean and the median of a distribution do not coincide, the median may be more appropriate to capture the *central tendency* of the distribution. The location shifts among the three education groups and between blacks and whites are considerably smaller when we examine the median rather than the mean. This difference raises concerns about using the conditional mean as an appropriate measure for modeling the location shift of asymmetric distributions.

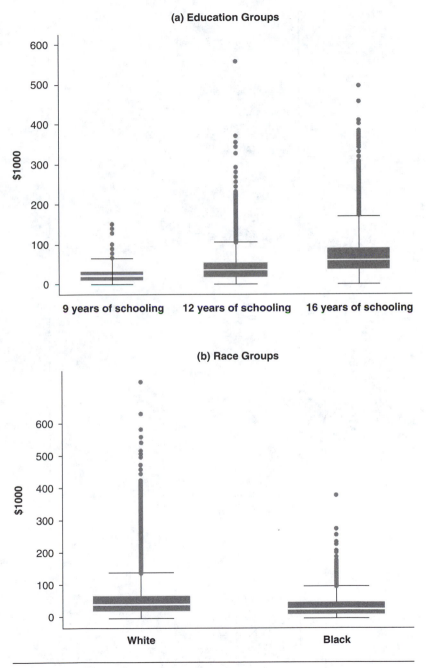

Figure 3.2   Box Graphs of Household Income

TABLE 3.1

Household Income Distribution:

Total, Education Groups, and Racial Groups

	Total	ED = 9	ED = 12	ED = 16	WHITE	BLACK
Mean	50,334	27,841	40,233	71,833	53,466	35,198
Quantile						
Median (.50th Quantile)	39,165	22,146	32,803	60,545	41,997	26,763
.10th Quantile	11,022	8,001	10,510	21,654	12,486	6,837
.25th Quantile	20,940	12,329	18,730	36,802	23,198	13,412
.75th Quantile	65,793	36,850	53,075	90,448	69,680	47,798
.90th Quantile	98,313	54,370	77,506	130,981	102,981	73,030
Quantile-Based Scale						
$(Q_{.75}-Q_{.25})$	44,853	24,521	34,344	53,646	46,482	34,386
$(Q_{.90}-Q_{.10})$	87,291	46,369	66,996	109,327	90,495	66,193
Quantile-Based Skewness						
$\dfrac{(Q_{.75}-Q_{.50})}{(Q_{.50}-Q_{.25})}-1$	.46	.50	.44	.26	.47	.58
$\dfrac{(Q_{.90}-Q_{.50})}{(Q_{.50}-Q_{.10})}-1$	1.10	1.28	1.01	.81	1.07	1.32

Conditional-Median and Quantile-Regression Models

With a skewed distribution, the median may become the more appropriate measure of central tendency; therefore, conditional-*median* regression, rather than conditional-*mean* regression, should be considered for the purpose of modeling location shifts. Conditional-median regression was proposed by Boscovich in the mid-18th century and was subsequently investigated by Laplace and Edgeworth. The median-regression model addresses the problematic conditional-mean estimates of the LRM. Median regression estimates the effect of a covariate on the conditional median, so it represents the central location even when the distribution is skewed.

To model both location shifts and shape shifts, Koenker and Bassett (1978) proposed a more general form than the median-regression model, the quantile-regression model (QRM). The QRM estimates the potential differential effect of a covariate on various quantiles in the conditional distribution, for example, a sequence of 19 equally distanced quantiles from the .05th quantile to the .95th quantile. With the median and the off-median quantiles, these 19 fitted regression lines capture the location shift (the line for the median), as well as scale and more complex shape shifts (the lines for off-median quantiles). In this way, the QRM estimates the differential effect of a covariate on the full distribution and accommodates heteroscedasticity.

Following Koenker and Bassett (1978), the QRM corresponding to the LRM in Equation 3.1 can be expressed as:

$$y_i = \beta_0^{(p)} + \beta_1^{(p)} x_i + \varepsilon_i^{(p)}, \qquad [3.2]$$

where $0 < p < 1$ indicates the proportion of the population having scores below the quantile at p. Recall that for LRM, the conditional mean of y_i given x_i is $E(y_i|x_i) = \beta_0 + \beta_1 x_i$, and this is equivalent to requiring that the error term ε_i have zero expectation. In contrast, for the corresponding QRM, we specify that the pth conditional *quantile* given x_i is $Q^{(p)}(y_i|x_i) = \beta_0^{(p)} + \beta_1^{(p)} x_i$. Thus, the conditional pth quantile is determined by the quantile-specific parameters, $\beta_0^{(p)}$ and $\beta_1^{(p)}$, and a specific value of the covariate x_i. As for the LRM, the QRM can be formulated equivalently with a statement about the error terms ε_i. Since the term $\beta_0^{(p)} + \beta_1^{(p)} x_i$ is a constant, we have $Q^{(p)}(y_i|x_i) = \beta_0^{(p)} + \beta_1^{(p)} x_i + Q^{(p)}(\varepsilon_i) = \beta_0^{(p)} + \beta_1^{(p)} x_i$, so an equivalent formulation of QRM requires that the pth quantile of the error term be zero.

It is important to note that for different values of the quantile p of interest, the error terms $\varepsilon_i^{(p)}$ for fixed i are related. In fact, replacing p by q in Equation 3.2 gives $y_i = \beta_0^{(q)} + \beta_1^{(q)} x_i + \varepsilon_i^{(q)}$, which leads to $\varepsilon_i^{(p)} - \varepsilon_i^{(q)} = (\beta_0^{(q)} - \beta_0^{(p)}) + x_i(\beta_1^{(q)} - \beta_1^{(p)})$, so that the two error terms differ by a constant given x_i. In other words, the distributions of $\varepsilon_i^{(p)}$ and $\varepsilon_i^{(q)}$ are shifts of one another. An important special case of QRM to consider is one in which the $\varepsilon_i^{(p)}$ for $i = 1, \ldots, n$ are independent and identically distributed; we refer to this as the i.i.d. case. In this situation, the qth quantile of $\varepsilon_i^{(p)}$ is a constant $c_{p,q}$ depending on p and q and not on i. Using Equation 3.2, we can express the qth conditional-quantile function as $Q^{(q)}(y_i|x_i) = Q^{(p)}(y_i|x_i) + c_{p,q}$.[2] We conclude that in the i.i.d. case, the conditional-quantile functions are simple shifts of one another, with the slopes $\beta_1^{(p)}$ taking a common value β_1. In other words, the i.i.d. assumption says that there are no shape shifts in the response variable.

Equation 3.2 dictates that unlike the LRM in Equation 3.1, which has only one conditional mean expressed by one equation, the QRM can have numerous conditional quantiles. Thus, numerous equations can be expressed in the form of Equation 3.2.[3] For example, if the QRM specifies 19 quantiles, the 19 equations yield 19 coefficients for x_i, one at each of the 19 conditional quantiles ($\beta_1^{.05}, \beta_1^{.10}, \ldots, \beta_1^{.95}$). The quantiles do not have to be equidistant, but in practice, having them at equal intervals makes them easier to interpret.

Fitting Equation 3.2 in our example yields estimates for the 19 conditional quantiles of income given education or race (see Tables 3.2 and 3.3). The coefficient for education grows monotonically from $1,019 at the .05th quantile to $8,385 at the .95th quantile. Similarly, the black effect is weaker at the lower quantiles than at the higher quantiles.

The selected conditional quantiles on 12 years of schooling are:

p	.05	.50	.95
$E(y_i \mid ED_i = 12)$	$7,976	$36,727	$111,268

and the selected conditional quantiles on blacks are:

p	.05	.50	.95
$E(y_i \mid BLACK_i = 1)$	$5,432	$26,764	$91,761

These results are very different from the conditional mean of the LRM. The conditional quantiles describe a conditional distribution, which can be used to summarize the location and shape shifts. Interpreting QRM estimates is a topic of Chapters 5 and 6.

Using a random sample of 1,000 households from the total sample and the fitted line based on the LRM, the left panel of Figure 3.3 presents the scatterplot of household income against the head of household's years of schooling. The single regression line indicates mean shifts, for example, a mean shift of $22,532 from 12 years of schooling to 16 years of schooling

TABLE 3.2
Quantile-Regression Estimates for Household Income on Education

	(1)	(2)	(3)	(4)	(5)	(6)	(7)	(8)	(9)	(10)	(11)	(12)	(13)	(14)	(15)	(16)	(17)	(18)	(19)
ED	1,019	1,617	2,023	2,434	2,750	3,107	3,397	3,657	3,948	4,208	4,418	4,676	4,905	5,214	5,557	5,870	6,373	6,885	8,385
	(28)	(31)	(40)	(39)	(44)	(51)	(57)	(64)	(66)	(72)	(81)	(92)	(88)	(102)	(127)	(138)	(195)	(274)	(463)
Constant	−4,252	−7,648	−9,170	−11,160	−12,056	−13,308	−13,783	−13,726	−14,026	−13,769	−12,546	−11,557	−9,914	−8,760	−7,371	−4,227	−1,748	4,755	10,648
	(380)	(424)	(547)	(527)	(593)	(693)	(764)	(866)	(884)	(969)	(1,084)	(1,226)	(1,169)	(1,358)	(1,690)	(1,828)	(2,582)	(3,619)	(6,101)

NOTE: Standard errors in parentheses.

TABLE 3.3
Quantile-Regression Estimates for Household Income on Race

	(1)	(2)	(3)	(4)	(5)	(6)	(7)	(8)	(9)	(10)	(11)	(12)	(13)	(14)	(15)	(16)	(17)	(18)	(19)
BLACK	−3,124	−5,649	−7,376	−8,848	−9,767	−11,232	−12,344	−13,349	−14,655	−15,233	−16,459	−17,417	−19,053	−20,314	−21,879	−22,914	−26,063	−29,951	−40,639
	(304)	(306)	(421)	(485)	(584)	(536)	(609)	(708)	(781)	(765)	(847)	(887)	(1,050)	(1,038)	(1,191)	(1,221)	(1,435)	(1,993)	(3,573)
Constant	8,556	12,486	16,088	19,718	23,198	26,832	30,354	34,024	38,047	41,997	46,635	51,515	56,613	62,738	69,680	77,870	87,996	102,981	132,400
	(115)	(116)	(159)	(183)	(220)	(202)	(230)	(268)	(295)	(289)	(320)	(335)	(397)	(392)	(450)	(461)	(542)	(753)	(1,350)

NOTE: Standard errors in parentheses.

$(5633 \cdot (16 - 12))$. However, this regression line does not capture shape shifts.

The right panel of Figure 3.3 shows the same scatterplot as in the left panel and the 19 quantile-regression lines. The .5th quantile (the median) fit captures the central location shifts, indicating a positive relationship between conditional-median income and education. The slope is $\$4,208$, shifting $\$16,832$ from 12 years of schooling to 16 years of schooling $(4208 \cdot (16 - 12))$. This shift is lower than the LRM mean shift.

In addition to the estimated location shifts, the other 18 quantile-regression lines provide information about shape shifts. These regression lines are positive, but with different slopes. The regression lines cluster tightly at low levels of education (e.g., 0–5 years of schooling) but deviate from each other more widely at higher levels of education (e.g., 16–20 years of

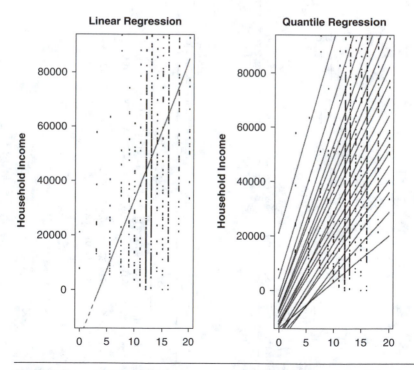

Figure 3.3   Effects of Education on the Conditional Mean and Conditional Quantiles of Household Income: A Random Sample of 1,000 Households

schooling). A shape shift is described by the tight cluster of the slopes at lower levels of education and the scattering of slopes at higher levels of education. For instance, the spread of the conditional income on 16 years of schooling (from \$12,052 for the .05th conditional quantile to \$144,808 for the .95th conditional quantile) is much wider than that on 12 years of schooling (from \$7,976 for the .05th conditional quantile to \$111,268 for the .95th conditional quantile). Thus, the off-median conditional quantiles isolate the location shift from the shape shift. This feature is crucial for determining the impact of a covariate on the location and shape shifts of the conditional distribution of the response, a topic discussed in Chapter 5 with the interpretation of the QRM results.

QR Estimation

We review least-squares estimation so as to place QR estimation in a familiar context. The least-squares estimator solves for the parameter estimates $\hat{\beta}_0$ and $\hat{\beta}_1$ by taking those values of the parameters that minimize the sum of squared residuals:

$$\min_i \sum_i (y_i - (\beta_0 + \beta_1 x_i))^2. \qquad [3.3]$$

If the LRM assumptions are correct, the fitted response function $\hat{\beta}_0 + \hat{\beta}_1$ approaches the population conditional mean $E(y\,|\,x)$ as the sample size goes to infinity. In Equation 3.3, the expression minimized is the sum of squared vertical distances between data points (x_i, y_i) and the fitted line $y = \hat{\beta}_0 + \hat{\beta}_1 x$.

A closed-form solution to the minimization problem is obtained by (a) taking partial derivatives of Equation 3.3 with respect to β_0 and β_1, respectively; (b) setting each partial derivative equal to zero; and (c) solving the resulting system of two equations with two unknowns. We then arrive at the two estimators:

$$\hat{\beta}_1 = \frac{\sum_i^n (x_i - \bar{x})(y_i - \bar{y})}{\sum_i^n (x_i - \bar{x})^2}, \quad \hat{\beta}_0 = \bar{y} - \hat{\beta}_1 \bar{x}.$$

A significant departure of the QR estimator from the LR estimator is that in the QR, the distance of points from a line is measured using a weighted sum of vertical distances (without squaring), where the weight is $1 - p$ for points below the fitted line and p for points above the line. Each choice for this proportion p, for example, $p = .10, .25, .50$, gives rise to a different fitted conditional-quantile function. The task is to find an estimator with the desired property for each possible p. The reader is reminded of the discussion in Chapter 2 where it was indicated that the mean of a distribution can be viewed as the point that minimizes the average squared distance over the population, whereas a quantile q can be viewed as the point that minimizes an average weighted distance, with weights depending on whether the point is above or below the value q.

For concreteness, we first consider the estimator for the median-regression model. In Chapter 2, we described how the median (m) of y can be viewed as the minimizing value of $E|y - m|$. For an analogous prescription in the median-regression case, we choose to minimize the sum of absolute residuals. In other words, we find the coefficients that minimize the sum of absolute residuals (the absolute distance from an observed value to its fitted value). The estimator solves for the βs by minimizing Equation 3.4:

$$\Sigma_i |y_i - \beta_0 - \beta_1 x_i|. \qquad [3.4]$$

Under appropriate model assumptions, as the sample size goes to infinity, we obtain the conditional median of y given x at the population level.

When expression Equation 3.4 is minimized, the resulting solution, which we refer to as the *median-regression line,* must pass through a pair of data points with half of the remaining data lying above the regression line and the other half falling below. That is, roughly half of the residuals are positive and half are negative. There are typically multiple lines with this property, and among these lines, the one that minimizes Equation 3.4 is the solution.

Algorithmic Details

In this subsection, we describe how the structure of the function Equation 3.4 makes it amenable to finding an algorithm for its minimization. Readers who are not interested in this topic can skip this section.

The left panel of Figure 3.4 shows eight hypothetical pairs of data points (x_i, y_i) and the 28 lines ($8(8 - 1)/2 = 28$) connecting a pair of these points is plotted. The dashed line is the fitted median-regression line, that is, the line that minimizes the sum of absolute vertical distance from all data points. Observe that of the six points not falling on the median-regression line, half of the points are below it and the other half are above it. Every line in the (x, y) plane takes the form $y = \beta_0 + \beta_1 x$ for some choice of intercept-slope pair (β_0, β_1), so that we have a correspondence between *lines* in the (x, y) plane and *points* in the (β_0, β_1) plane. The right panel of Figure 3.4 shows a plot in the (β_0, β_1) plane that contains a point corresponding to every line in the left panel. In particular, the solid circle shown in the right panel corresponds to the median-regression line in the left panel.

In addition, if a line with intercept and slope (β_0, β_1) passes through a given point (x_i, y_i), then $y_i = \beta_0 + \beta_1 x_i$, so that (β_0, β_1) lies on the line $\beta_1 = (y_i/x_i) - (1/x_i)\beta_0$. Thus, we have established a correspondence between points in the (x, y) plane and lines in the (β_0, β_1) plane and vice versa, a phenomenon referred to as *point/line duality* (Edgeworth, 1888).

The eight lines shown in the right panel of Figure 3.4 correspond to the eight data points in the left panel. These lines divide the (β_0, β_1) plane into polygonal regions. An example of such a region is shaded in Figure 3.4. In any one of these regions, the points correspond to a family of lines in the (x, y) plane, all of which divide the data set into two sets in exactly the same way (meaning that the data points above one line are the same as the points above the other). Consequently, the function of (β_0, β_1) that we seek to minimize in Equation 3.4 is linear in each region, so that this function is convex with a graph that forms a polyhedral surface, which is plotted from two different angles in Figure 3.5 for our example. The vertices,

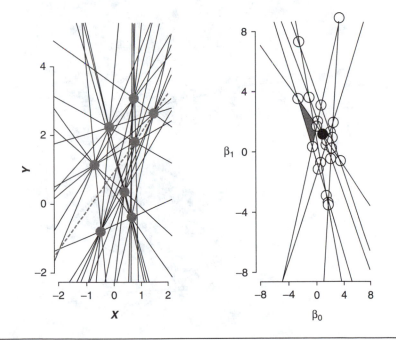

Figure 3.4   An Illustration of Point/Line Duality

edges, and facets of the surface project to points, line segments, and regions, respectively, in the (β_0, β_1) plane shown in the right-hand panel of Figure 3.4. Using the point/line duality correspondence, each vertex corresponds to a line connecting a pair of data points. An edge connecting two vertices in the surface corresponds to a pair of such lines, where one of the data points defining the first line is replaced by another data point, and the remaining points maintain their position (above or below) relative to both lines.

An algorithm for minimization of the sum of absolute distances in Equation 3.4, one thus leading to the median-regression coefficients $(\hat{\beta}_0, \hat{\beta}_1)$, can be based on exterior-point algorithms for solving linear-programming problems. Starting at any one of the points (β_0, β_1) corresponding to a vertex, the minimization is achieved by iteratively moving from vertex to

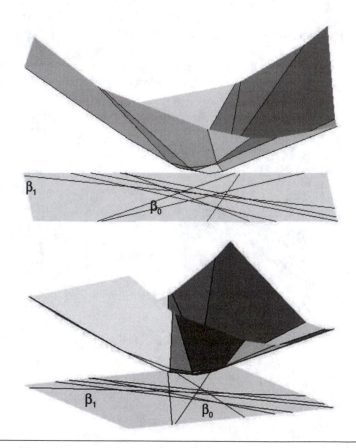

Figure 3.5   Polyhedral Surface and Its Projection

vertex along the edges of the polyhedral surface, choosing at each vertex the path of the steepest descent until arriving at the minimum. Using the correspondence described in the previous paragraph, we iteratively move from line to line defined by pairs of data points, at each step deciding which new data point to swap with one of the two current ones by picking the one that leads to the smallest value in Equation 3.4. The minimum sum of absolute errors is attained at the point in the (β_0, β_1) plane below the lowest vertex of the surface. A simple argument involving the directional derivative with respect to β_0 (similar to the one in Chapter 2 showing that the median is the solution to a minimization problem) leads to the conclusion that the same number of data points lie above the median-regression line as lie below it.

The median-regression estimator can be generalized to allow for pth quantile-regression estimators (Koenker & d'Orey, 1987). Recall from the discussion in Chapter 2 that the pth quantile of a univariate sample $y_1, \ldots, y_n$ distribution is the value q that minimizes the sum of weighted distances from the sample points, where points below q receive a weight of $1 - p$ and points above q receive a weight of p. In a similar manner, we define the pth quantile-regression estimators $\hat{\beta}_0^{(p)}$ and $\hat{\beta}_1^{(p)}$ as the values that minimize the weighted sum of distances between fitted values $\hat{y}_i = \hat{\beta}_0^{(p)} + \hat{\beta}_1^{(p)} x_i$ and the y_i, where we use a weight of $1 - p$ if the fitted value underpredicts the observed value y_i and a weight of p otherwise. In other words, we seek to minimize a weighted sum of residuals $y_i - \hat{y}_i$ where positive residuals receive a weight of p and negative residuals receive a weight of $1 - p$. Formally, the pth quantile-regression estimators $\hat{\beta}_0^{(p)}$ and $\hat{\beta}_1^{(p)}$ are chosen to minimize

$$\sum_{i=1}^{n} d_p(y_i, \hat{y}_i) = p \sum_{y_i \geq \beta_0^{(p)} + \beta_1^{(p)} x_i} |y_i - \beta_0^{(p)} - \beta_1^{(p)} x_i| + (1 - p)$$

$$\sum_{y_i < \beta_0^{(p)} + \beta_1^{(p)} x_i} |y_i - \beta_0^{(p)} - \beta_1^{(p)} x_i|, \qquad [3.5]$$

where d_p is the distance introduced in Chapter 2. Thus, unlike Equation 3.4, which states that the negative residuals are given the same importance as the positive residuals, Equation 3.5 assigns different weights to positive and negative residuals. Observe that in Equation 3.5, the first sum is the sum of vertical distances of data points from the line $y = \beta_0^{(p)} + \beta_1^{(p)} x$, for points lying above the line. The second is a similar sum over all data points lying below the line.

Observe that, contrary to a common misconception, the estimation of coefficients for each quantile regression is based on the weighted data of the whole sample, not just the portion of the sample at that quantile.

An algorithm for computing the quantile-regression coefficients $\hat{\beta}_0^{(p)}$ and $\hat{\beta}_1^{(p)}$ can be developed along lines similar to those outlined for the median-regression coefficients. The pth quantile-regression estimator has a similar property to one stated for the median-regression estimator: The proportion of data points lying below the fitted line $y = \hat{\beta}_0^{(p)} + \hat{\beta}_1^{(p)} x$ is p, and the proportion lying above is $1 - p$.

For example, when we estimate the coefficients for the .10th quantile-regression line, the observations below the line are given a weight of .90 and the ones above the line receive a smaller weight of .10. As a result, 90% of the data points (x_i, y_i) lie above the fitted line leading to positive residuals, and 10% lie below the line and thus have negative residuals. Conversely, to estimate the coefficients for the .90th quantile regression, points below the line are given a weight of .10, and the rest have a weight of .90; as a result, 90% of observations have negative residuals and the remaining 10% have positive residuals.

Transformation and Equivariance

In analyzing a response variable, researchers often transform the scale to aid interpretation or to attain a better model fit. Equivariance properties of models and estimates refer to situations when, if the data are transformed, the models or estimates undergo the same transformation. Knowledge of equivariance properties helps us to reinterpret fitted models when we transform the response variable.

For any linear transformation of the response variable, that is, the addition of a constant to y or the multiplication of y by a constant, the conditional mean of the LRM can be exactly transformed. The basis for this statement is the fact that for any choice of constants a and c, we can write

$$E(c + ay|x) = c + aE(y|x). \qquad [3.6]$$

For example, if every household in the population received $500 from the government, the conditional mean would also be increased by $500 (the new intercept would be increased by $500). When the $1 unit of income is transformed to the $1,000 unit, the conditional mean in the $1 unit is increased by 1,000 times as well (the intercept and the slope are both multiplied by 1,000 to be on the dollar scale). Similarly, if the dollar unit for wage rate is transformed to the cent unit, the conditional mean (the intercept and the slope) is divided by 100 to be on the dollar scale again. This property is termed *linear equivariance* because the linear transformation is the same for the dependent variable and the conditional mean. The QRM also has this property:

$$Q^{(p)}(c + ay|x) = c + a(Q^{(p)}[y \mid x]), \qquad [3.7]$$

provided that a is a positive constant. If a is negative, we have $Q^{(p)}(c + ay \mid x) = c + a(Q^{(1-p)}[y|x])$ because the order is reversed.

Situations often arise in which nonlinear transformation is desired. Log transformations are frequently used to address the right-skewness of a distribution. Other transformations are considered in order to make a distribution appear more normal or to achieve a better model fit.

Log transformations are also introduced in order to model a covariate's effect in relative terms (e.g., percentage changes). In other words, the effect of a covariate is viewed on a multiplicative scale rather than on an additive one. In our example, the effects of education or race were previously expressed in additive terms (the dollar unit), and it may be desirable to measure an effect in multiplicative terms, for example, in terms of percentage changes. For example, we can ask: What is the percentage change in conditional-mean income brought about by one more year of schooling? The coefficient for education in a log income equation (multiplied by 100) approximates the percentage change in conditional-mean income brought about by one more year of schooling. However, under the LRM, the conditional mean of log income is not the same as the log of conditional-mean income. Estimating two LRMs using income and log income yields two fitted models:

$$\hat{y} = -23{,}127 + 5{,}633ED, \ \log \hat{y} = 8.982 + .115ED.$$

The result from the log income model suggests that one more year of education increases the conditional-mean income by about 11.5%.[4] The conditional mean of the income model at 10 years of schooling is $33,203, the log of which becomes 8.108. The conditional mean of the log income model at the same schooling level is 10.062, a much larger figure than the log of the conditional mean of income (8.108). While the log transformation of a response in the LRM allows an interpretation of LRM estimates as a percentage change, the conditional mean of the response in absolute terms is impossible to obtain from the conditional mean on the log scale:

$$E(\log y \mid x) \neq \log [E(y \mid x)] \text{ and } E(y_i \mid x_i) \neq e^{E[\log y_i \mid x_i]}. \qquad [3.8]$$

Specifically, if our aim is to estimate the education effect in absolute terms, we use the income model, whereas for the impact of education in relative terms, we use the log income model. Although the two objectives are related to each other, the conditional means of the two models are not related through any simple transformation.[5] Thus, it would be a mistake to use the log income results to make conclusions about the distribution of income (though this is a widely used practice).

The log transformation is one member of the family of *monotone* transformations, that is, transformations that preserve order. Formally, a transformation h is a monotone if $h(y) < h(y')$ whenever $y < y'$. For variables taking positive values, the power transformation $h(y) = y^\phi$ is monotone for a fixed positive value of the constant ϕ. As a result of nonlinearity, when we apply a monotone transformation, the degree to which the transformation changes the value of y can differ from one value of y to the next. While the property in Equation 3.6 holds for linear functions, it is not the case for general monotone functions, that is, $E(h(y)|x) \neq h(E(y_i|x_i))$. Generally speaking, the "monotone equivariance" property fails to hold for conditional means, so that LRMs do not possess monotone equivariance.

By contrast, the conditional quantiles do possess monotone equivariance; that is, for a monotone function h, we have

$$Q^{(p)}(h(y)|x) = h(Q^{(p)}[y|x]). \qquad [3.9]$$

This property follows immediately from the version of monotone equivariance stated for univariate quantiles in Chapter 2. In particular, a conditional quantile of log y is the log of the conditional quantile of y:

$$Q^{(p)}(\log(y)|x) = \log(Q^{(p)}[y|x]), \qquad [3.10]$$

and equivalently,

$$Q^{(p)}(y|x) = e^{Q^{(p)}[\log(y)|x]}, \qquad [3.11]$$

so that we are able to reinterpret fitted quantile-regression models for untransformed variables to quantile-regression models for transformed variables. In other words, assuming a perfect fit for the pth quantile function of the form $Q^{(p)}(y|x) = \beta_0 + \beta_1 x$, we have $Q^{(p)}(\log y|x) = \log(\beta_0 + \beta_1 x)$, so that we can use the impact of a covariate expressed in absolute terms to describe the impact of a covariate in relative terms and vice versa.

Take the conditional median as an example:

$$Q^{(.50)}(y_i|ED_i) = -13769 + 4208ED_i, \quad Q^{(.50)}(\log(y_i)|ED_i) = 8.966 + .123ED_i.$$

The conditional median of income at 10 years of schooling is $28,311. The log of this conditional median, 10.251, is similar to the conditional median of the log income equation at the same education level, 10.196. Correspondingly, when moving from log to raw scale, in absolute terms, the conditional median at 10 years of schooling from the log income equation is $e^{10.916} = 28,481$.

The QRM's monotone equivariance is particularly important for research involving skewed distributions. While the original distribution is distorted by the reverse transformation of log-scale estimates if the LRM is used, the original distribution is preserved if the QRM is used. A covariate's effect on the response variable in terms of percentage change is often used in inequality research. Hence, the monotone equivariance property allows researchers to achieve both goals: measuring percentage change caused by a unit change in the covariate and measuring the impact of this change on the location and shape of the raw-scale conditional distribution.

Robustness

Robustness refers to insensitivity to outliers and to the violation of model assumptions concerning the data y. Outliers are defined as some values of y that do not follow the relationship for the majority values. Under the LRM, estimates can be sensitive to outliers. Earlier in the first section of this chapter, we presented an example showing how outliers of income distribution distort the mean and the conditional mean. The high sensitivity of the LRM to outliers has been widely recognized. However, the practice of eliminating outliers does not satisfy the objective of much social-science research, particularly inequality research.

In contrast, the QRM estimates are not sensitive to outliers.[6] This robustness arises because of the nature of the distance function in Equation 3.5 that is minimized, and we can state a property of quantile-regression estimates that is similar to a statement made in Chapter 2 about univariate quantiles. If we modify the value of the response variable for a data point lying above (or below) the fitted quantile-regression line, as long as that data point remains above (or below) the line, the fitted quantile-regression line remains unchanged. Stated another way, if we modify values of the response variable without changing the sign of the residual, the fitted line remains the same. In this way, as for univariate quantiles, the influence of outliers is quite limited.

In addition, since the covariance matrix of the estimates is calculated under the normality assumption, the LRM's normality assumption is necessary for obtaining the inferential statistics of the LRM. Violation of the normality assumption can cause inaccuracy in standard errors. The QRM is robust to distributional assumptions because the estimator weighs the local behavior of the distribution near the specific quantile more than the remote behavior of the distribution. The QRM's inferential statistics can be distribution free (a topic discussed in Chapter 4). This robustness is important in studying phenomena of highly skewed distributions such as income, wealth, educational, and health outcomes.

Summary

This chapter introduces the basics of the quantile-regression model in comparison with the linear-regression model, including the model setup, the estimation, and the properties of estimates. The QRM inherits many of the properties of sample quantiles introduced in Chapter 2. We explain how LRM is inadequate for revealing certain types of effects of covariates on the distribution of a response variable. We also highlight some of the key features of QRM. We present many of the important differences between the QRM and the LRM, namely, (a) multiple-quantile-regression fits versus single-linear-regression fits to data; (b) quantile-regression estimation that minimizes a weighted sum of absolute values of residuals as opposed to minimizing the sum of squares in least-squares estimation; and (c) the monotone equivariance and robustness to distributional assumptions in conditional quantiles versus the lack of these properties in the conditional mean. With these basics, we are now ready to move on to the topic of QRM inference.

Notes

1. The data are drawn from the 2001 panel of the Survey of Income and Program Participation (SIPP). Household income is the annual income in 2001. The analytic sample for Chapters 3 through 5 includes 19,390 white households and 3,243 black households.

2. $Q^{(q)}(y_i \mid x_i) = Q^{(q)}(\beta_0^{(p)} + x_i\beta_1^{(p)} + \varepsilon_i^{(p)}) = \beta_0^{(p)} + x_i\beta_1^{(p)} + Q^{(q)}(\varepsilon_i^{(p)}) = Q^{(p)}(y_i \mid x_i) + c_{p,q}$.

3. The number of distinct quantile solutions, however, is bounded by the finite sample size.

4. Precisely, the percentage change is $100(e^{.115}-1) = 12.2\%$.

5. The conditional mean is proportional to the exponential of the linear predictor (Manning, 1998). For example, if the errors are normally distributed $N(0, \sigma_\varepsilon^2)$, then $E(y_i \mid x_i) = e^{\beta_0 + \beta_1 x_i + 0.5\sigma_\varepsilon^2}$. The term $e^{0.5\sigma_\varepsilon^2}$ is sometimes called the smearing factor.

6. Note that this robustness does not apply to outliers of covariates.

4. QUANTILE-REGRESSION INFERENCE

Chapter 3 covered the topic of parameter estimation. We now turn to the topic of inferential statistics, specifically standard errors and confidence intervals for coefficient estimates from the QRM. We begin with an overview of inference in the LRM, discussing the exact finite sample and asymptotic distributions of quantities used in the construction of confidence intervals and hypothesis tests. Then, we introduce the corresponding asymptotic procedure for the QRM. Next, we introduce the bootstrap procedure for the QRM, which allows for inference about QRM coefficients. The bootstrap procedure is preferable to the asymptotic because the assumptions for the asymptotic procedure usually do not hold, and even if these assumptions are satisfied, it is complicated to solve for the standard error of the constructed scale and skewness shifts. The bootstrap procedure offers the flexibility to obtain the standard error and confidence interval for any estimates and combinations of estimates. The last section of this chapter discusses the topics of goodness of fit and model checking.

Standard Errors and Confidence Intervals for the LRM

We begin with an overview of inference for coefficients in the LRM expressed in the form $y_i = \sum_{j=1}^{k} \beta_j x_j^{(i)} + \varepsilon_i$ under ideal modeling assumptions, which state that errors ε_i are independently and identically (i.i.d.) normally distributed with mean 0 and a constant variance σ^2, so that exact distributions can be derived. The expression $x_j^{(i)}$ is used to denote the value of the jth covariate for the ith sampled individual. It will be helpful below to think of $x^{(i)}$, the vector of covariate values for the ith individual, as a (row) k-vector.

The usual estimator of the error variance is given by $\hat{\sigma}^2 = RSS/(n-k)$, where RSS denotes the residual sum of squares and k is the number of predictor variables (including the intercept term) used in the fitted model. Letting the $n \times k$ matrix of predictor variable values be denoted by X (so that the ith row is $x^{(i)}$, the covariate values for the ith individual), the joint distribution of the least-squares estimator $\hat{\beta}$ of the vector of regression coefficients is multivariate normal, with the mean being the true β and the covariance matrix given by $\sigma^2(X^tX)^{-1}$. As a consequence, an individual coefficient estimator $\hat{\beta}_j$ has a normal distribution, with the mean being the true β_j, and a variance of $\delta_j\sigma^2$, where δ_j denotes the jth diagonal entry of the matrix $(X^tX)^{-1}$. Thus, we estimate the variance of $\hat{\beta}_j$ using $\delta_j\hat{\sigma}^2$.

Naturally, we estimate the standard deviation of the estimator by the square root of this estimator and refer to this as the standard error of $\hat{\beta}_j$ (denoted by $s_{\hat{\beta}_j}$). As a consequence of the assumptions about the error distribution, the quantity $(\hat{\beta}_j - \beta_j)/s_{\hat{\beta}_j}$ is distributed as Student's t with $n - k$ degrees of freedom. This allows us to form the standard $100(1-\alpha)\%$ confidence interval for β_j of the form $\hat{\beta}_j \pm t_{\alpha/2}s_{\hat{\beta}_j}$, as well as the test at level α for whether the jth covariate significantly affects the dependent variable by rejecting the null hypothesis H_0: $\beta_j = 0$ if $|\hat{\beta}_j/s_{\hat{\beta}_j}| > t_{\alpha/2}$.

These exact results, then, remain valid approximately for large samples, even when we relax normality assumption of normal errors. In that case, the quantity $(\hat{\beta}_j - \beta_j)/s_{\hat{\beta}_j}$ has an approximate standard normal distribution. Thus, in the tests and confidence intervals described above, one would typically replace the upper $\alpha/2$ critical point of the t distribution by $z_{\alpha/2}$, the upper $\alpha/2$ critical point of the standard normal distribution.

Table 4.1 shows the results for a linear-regression model fit where income is a function of two predictor variables, *ED* and *WHITE*. Estimated coefficients are given together with their standard errors in parentheses. For example, for *ED,* the standard error is estimated as $98. The coefficient for *WHITE* also has a small standard error of $777.

TABLE 4.1

Asymptotic Standard Error of

Linear-Regression Estimate for Income

Variable	Income
ED	6,294**
	(98)
WHITE	11,317**
	(777)
R-squared	0.16

NOTE: ** $p < .01$

Standard Errors and Confidence Intervals for the QRM

We wish to make inferences for the coefficients $\beta^{(p)}$ in the QRM written in the form $Q^{(p)}(y_i|x^{(i)}) = \sum_{j=1}^{k} \beta_j^{(p)}x_j^{(i)}$. As in Chapter 3, an equivalent form of this model states that $y_i = \sum_{j=1}^{k} \beta_j^{(p)}x_j^{(i)} + \varepsilon_i^{(p)}$, where the $\varepsilon_i^{(p)}$ have a common distribution whose pth quantile is zero. Inference for a coefficient $\beta_j^{(p)}$ will be in the form of a confidence interval or hypothesis test based on some measure of standard error $s_{\hat{\beta}_j^{(p)}}$ of $\hat{\beta}_j^{(p)}$, as in the LRM setting. This standard error will have the property that asymptotically, the quantity $(\hat{\beta}_j^{(p)}-\beta_j^{(p)})/s_{\hat{\beta}_j^{(p)}}$ has a standard normal distribution.

Standard errors for the QRM are considerably simpler and easier to describe under the i.i.d. model presented in Chapter 3. In this case, the asymptotic covariance matrix for $\hat{\beta}^{(p)}$ takes the form

$$\Sigma_{\hat{\beta}(p)} = \frac{p(1-p)}{n} \cdot \frac{1}{f_{\varepsilon^{(p)}}(0)^2}(X^tX)^{-1}. \qquad [4.1]$$

The term $f_{\varepsilon^{(p)}}(0)$ appearing in Equation 4.1 is the probability density of the error term $\varepsilon^{(p)}$ evaluated at the pth quantile of the error distribution.[1] As in the LRM, the covariance matrix is a scalar multiple of the $(X^tX)^{-1}$ matrix. However, in the QRM, the multiplier $\frac{p(1-p)}{n} \cdot \frac{1}{f_{\varepsilon^{(p)}}(0)^2}$ is the asymptotic variance of a sample quantile based on a (univariate) sample $\varepsilon_1^{(p)}, \ldots, \varepsilon_n^{(p)}$. The density term appearing in this expression is unknown and needs to be estimated just as in the univariate case, and the procedure described in Chapter 2 for estimation of the corresponding term is easily adapted to the present situation. The quantity $\frac{1}{f_{\varepsilon^{(p)}}} = \frac{d}{dp}Q^{(p)}(\varepsilon^{(p)})$ can be estimated using a difference quotient $\frac{1}{2h}(\hat{Q}^{(p)}(p+h) - \hat{Q}^{(p)}(p-h))$, where the sample quantiles $\hat{Q}(p \pm h)$ are based on the residuals $\hat{\varepsilon}_i^{(p)} = y_i \sum_{j=1}^{k}\hat{\beta}_j^{(p)}x_j^{(i)}, i = 1, \ldots, n$ for the fitted QRM model. The choice of h to use is a delicate one, and Koenker (2005) describes a couple of approaches to choosing h.

It is more complex to deal with the *non-i.i.d.* case. In this case, the $\varepsilon_i^{(p)}$ no longer have a common distribution, but all of these distributions still have a pth quantile of zero. To handle this noncommon distribution, it becomes necessary to introduce a *weighted* version (D_1 below) of the X^tX matrix.

All of the *analytic* methods for obtaining approximate standard errors in the QRM are derived from a general result described in Koenker (2005) giving a multivariate normal approximation to the joint distribution of the coefficient estimates $\hat{\beta}_j^{(p)}$. This distribution has a mean with components that are the true coefficients and a covariance matrix of the form: $\Sigma_{\beta(p)} = \frac{p(1-p)}{n}D_1^{-1}D_0D_1^{-1}$, where

$$D_0 = \lim_{n\to\infty}\frac{1}{n}\sum_{i=1}^{n}x^{(i)t}x^{(i)}, \text{ and } D_1 = \lim_{n\to\infty}\frac{1}{n}\sum_{i=1}^{n}w_ix^{(i)t}x^{(i)}, \qquad [4.2]$$

where $x^{(i)}$ is the ith row of X with dimension of $1 \times k$. Here the terms D_0 and D_1 are $k \times k$ matrices. The weight $w_i = f_{\varepsilon_i^{(p)}}(0)$, with the probability density function $\varepsilon_i^{(p)}$ evaluated at 0 (which is the pth conditional quantile of $\varepsilon_i^{(p)}$). Thus, we can think of the sum in the expression for D_1 as being $\tilde{X}^t\tilde{X}$, where $\tilde{X}$ is obtained from X by multiplying the ith row by $\sqrt{w_i}$. Mild conditions can be given under which convergence in Equation 4.1 is to positive definite matrices D_i. As in the i.i.d. case, we see the asymptotic distribution of

$\hat{\beta}^{(p)}$ on the conditional-density function evaluated at the quantile of interest. However, since the $\varepsilon_i^{(p)}$ are not identically distributed, these terms differ with i, leading to different weights. Since the density function is unknown, it becomes necessary to estimate the weights w_i appearing in Equation 4.2. Two methods for producing estimates $\hat{w}_i$ of the weights are described in Koenker (2005). Whatever method is employed, the covariance matrix for $\hat{\beta}^{(p)}$ is estimated as $\hat{\Sigma} = \frac{p(1-p)}{n} \hat{D}_1^{-1} \hat{D}_0 \hat{D}_1^{-1}$, where

$$\hat{D}_0 = \frac{1}{n} \sum_{i=1}^{n} x^{(i)t} x^{(i)}, \text{ and } \hat{D}_1 = \frac{1}{n} \sum_{i=1}^{n} \hat{w}_i x^{(i)t} x^{(i)}. \qquad [4.3]$$

An estimated standard error for an individual coefficient estimator $\hat{\beta}_j^{(p)}$ is obtained by taking the square root of the corresponding diagonal element of the estimated covariance matrix $\hat{\Sigma}$. As in the i.i.d. case, we are now able to test hypotheses about the effects of the covariates on the dependent variable, and to obtain confidence intervals for the quantile-regression coefficients.

Table 4.2 shows the asymptotic and bootstrap standard error of estimates in a two-covariate QRM for the .05th and .95th income quantiles, respectively. The asymptotic and bootstrap errors differ moderately but lead to the same conclusion about the effect of *ED* and *WHITE*. The point estimate for *ED* is $1,130, and the standard error is $36 at the .05th quantile. The corresponding numbers at the .95th quantile are $9,575 and $605, respectively. The coefficient for *WHITE* is $3,197 with a standard error of $359 at the .05th quantile, and $17,484 with a standard error of $2,895 at the .95th quantile. Confidence intervals can be obtained using the standard errors.

TABLE 4.2

Quantile-Regression Model of Income With
Asymptotic and 500 Resample Bootstrap Standard Errors

	P	
Variable	*.05*	*.95*
ED	1,130	9,575
	(36)	(605)
	[80]	[268]
WHITE	3,197	17,484
	(359)	(2,895)
	[265]	[2,280]

NOTE: Asymptotic standard errors are in parentheses and bootstrap standard errors are in brackets.

Table 4.2 shows that the positive effects of *ED* and *WHITE* are statistically significant for the two extreme quantiles. However, whether the effect of a covariate differs significantly across quantiles needs to be tested. These tests require a covariance matrix of the coefficients across quantiles. As we discussed above, estimating the variance of the error in the QRM is more complicated than in the LRM; therefore, the covariance of coefficients from multiple QRMs would be even more complicated, making a closed-form solution practically impossible. Thus, we need an alternative method to estimate the covariance of coefficients across quantiles, which will be discussed in the next section.

The more important concern about the asymptotic standard error is that the i.i.d. assumption of errors is unlikely to hold. The often-observed skewness and outliers make the error distribution depart from i.i.d. Standard large-sample approximations have been found to be highly sensitive to minor deviations from the i.i.d. error assumption. Thus, asymptotic procedures based on strong parametric assumptions may be inappropriate for performing hypothesis testing and for estimating the confidence intervals (Koenker, 1994). Alternative methods that do not make the i.i.d. assumption are more robust and practical (e.g., Kocherginsky, He, & Mu, 2005). In order to obtain robust results, a statistical technique that is applicable regardless of the form of the probability density function for the response variable and the error is desirable. In other words, this alternative method should make no assumption about the distribution of the response. A good candidate is the *bootstrap* method.

The Bootstrap Method for the QRM

An alternative to the asymptotic method described in the previous section is to apply the bootstrap approach. The bootstrap method is a Monte-Carlo method for estimating the sampling distribution of a parameter estimate that is calculated from a sample of size n from some population. When ordinary Monte-Carlo simulation is used to approximate the sampling distribution, the population distribution is assumed to be known, samples of size n are drawn from that distribution, and each sample is used to calculate a parameter estimate. The *empirical* distribution of these calculated parameter estimates is then used as an approximation to the desired sampling distribution. In particular, the standard error of the estimate can be estimated using standard deviation of the sample of parameter estimates.

The bootstrap approach, introduced by Efron (1979), differs from ordinary Monte-Carlo simulation. Instead of drawing samples from a hypothetical distribution, we draw samples of size n *with replacement* from the actual observed data set. The number of resamples, denoted by *M,* is usually between 50 and 200 for estimating a standard deviation and between 500 and 2,000 for a confidence interval. Although each resample will have the same number of elements as the original sample, it could include some of the original data points more than once while excluding others. Therefore, each of these resamples will randomly depart from the original sample.

To illustrate the bootstrap with a concrete example, consider the estimation of the 25th percentile $Q^{(.25)}$ of a population based on sample 25th percentile $\hat{Q}^{(.25)}$ for a sample $y_1, \ldots, y_n$. We would like to estimate the standard error of this estimate. One approach to this is to use the large-sample approximation to the variance of $\hat{Q}^{(p)}$ given in Chapter 2. This gives

$$\sqrt{\frac{p(1-p)}{nf(Q^{(p)})^2}} = \sqrt{\frac{(1/4)(3/4)}{nf(Q^{(p)})^2}} = \frac{\sqrt{3}}{4\sqrt{nf(Q^{(.25)})}}$$ as an approximation to the standard

deviation of $\hat{Q}^{(.25)}$, where f denotes the population-density function. Since the density is unknown, it becomes necessary to estimate it, and as in the beginning of this chapter, we can estimate the term $1/f(\hat{Q}^{(.25)})$ using $(\hat{Q}^{(.25+h)} - \hat{Q}^{(.25-h)})/(2h)$ for some appropriate choice of the constant h.

The bootstrap approach to this problem is somewhat more direct: We draw a large number of samples of size n with replacement from the original data set. Each of these samples is referred to as a *bootstrap* sample. For the *m*th *bootstrap* sample $\tilde{y}_1^{(m)}, \ldots, \tilde{y}_n^{(m)}$, we compute a value $\hat{Q}_m^{(25)}$ Repeating this large number $M(50$ to $200)$ times leads to a sample $\hat{Q}_m^{(.25)}, m = 1, \ldots, M$, which we treat as drawn from the sampling distribution of $\hat{Q}^{(.25)}$. We then use the standard deviation s_{boot} of the $\hat{Q}_m^{(.25)}, m = 1, \ldots, M$ to estimate the desired standard deviation.

The bootstrap estimates can also be used to form an approximate confidence interval for the desired population 25th percentile. A variety of approaches are available for this. One is to make use of the original estimate $\hat{Q}^{(.25)}$ from the sample, its estimated standard error s_{boot}, and normal approximation to give a $100(1 - \alpha)\%$ confidence interval of the form $\hat{Q}^{(.25)} \pm z_{\alpha/2} s_{boot}$.

Another alternative is to make use of the empirical quantiles of the sample of bootstrap estimates. For a bootstrap 95% confidence interval, we take the endpoints of the interval to be the empirical .025th and .975th quantiles of the sample bootstrap estimates. To be more specific, if we order the bootstrap estimates $\hat{Q}_1^{(.25)}, \ldots, \hat{Q}_{1000}^{(.25)}$ from smallest to largest to give order statistics $\hat{Q}_{(1)}^{(.25)}, \ldots, \hat{Q}_{(1000)}^{(.25)}$, we take the confidence interval to be $\left[\hat{Q}_{(50)}^{(.25)}, \hat{Q}_{(951)}^{(.25)}\right]$. A similar construction is possible for a confidence interval with any desired coverage probability.

Extending this idea to the QRM, we wish to estimate standard errors of quantile-regression parameter estimates $\beta^{(p)} = (\beta_1^{(p)}, \ldots, \beta_k^{(p)})$, which are estimated based on data consisting of sample covariate-response pairs (x_i, y_i), $i = 1, \ldots, n$. The (x, y)-pair bootstrap refers to the approach in which bootstrap samples of size n are obtained by sampling with replacement from these pairs, that is, the micro units (individuals with their x, y data). Identical copies of a data pair in the sample are counted according to their multiplicity, so that a copy appearing k times would be k times more likely to be sampled.

Each bootstrap sample gives rise to a parameter estimate, and we estimate the standard error s_{boot} of a particular coefficient estimate $\hat{\beta}_i^{(p)}$ by taking the standard deviation of the M bootstrap estimates. The bootstrap estimates can be used to produce a confidence interval for an individual quantile regression parameter $\beta_i^{(p)}$ in various ways. One method is to make use of the standard error estimate and normal approximation: $\hat{\beta}_i^{(p)} \pm z_{\alpha/2} s_{boot}$. Alternatively, we can base a confidence interval on sample quantiles. For example, a 95% confidence interval of $\hat{\beta}_i^{(p)}$ is from the 2.5th percentile to the 97.5th percentile of the sample consisting of M bootstrap estimates $\hat{\beta}_m^p$.

Multiple QRMs based, for instance, on 19 equispaced quantiles ($p = .05, \ldots, .95$) can be considered collectively. We can estimate the covariance between all possible quantile-regression coefficients over the 19 models. For example, when the model being fitted contains an intercept parameter $\hat{\beta}_1^{(p)}$ and coefficients corresponding to two covariates $\hat{\beta}_2^{(p)}$ and $\hat{\beta}_3^{(p)}$, we have $3 \times 19 = 57$ estimated coefficients, yielding a 57×57 covariance matrix. This matrix provides not only the variance for the coefficient of each covariate at each quantile (e.g., $Var(\hat{\beta}_1^{(.05)})$ and $Var(\hat{\beta}_1^{(.50)})$) but also the covariance of estimates at different quantiles for the same covariate (e.g., $Cov(\hat{\beta}_1^{(.05)}, \hat{\beta}_1^{(.50)})$).

With both variance and covariance estimated, we can perform hypotheses testing on the equivalence of a pair of coefficients $\beta_i^{(p)}$ and $\beta_i^{(q)}$ corresponding to the same covariate but across distinct quantiles p and q using a Wald statistic:

$$\text{Wald statistic} = \frac{(\hat{\beta}_j^{(p)} - \hat{\beta}_j^{(q)})^2}{\hat{\sigma}^2_{\hat{\beta}_j^{(p)} - \hat{\beta}_j^{(q)}}}. \qquad [4.4]$$

The term $\hat{\sigma}^2_{\beta_j^{(p)} - \beta_j^{(q)}}$ in the denominator is the estimated variance of the difference $\hat{\beta}_j^{(p)} - \hat{\beta}_j^{(q)}$, which is obtained by using the following equality and substituting the estimated variances and covariances on the right-hand side:

$$Var(\hat{\beta}_j^{(p)} - \hat{\beta}_j^{(q)}) = Var(\hat{\beta}_j^{(p)}) + Var(\hat{\beta}_j^{(q)}) - 2Cov(\hat{\beta}_j^{(p)}, \hat{\beta}_j^{(q)}). \qquad [4.5]$$

Under the null hypothesis, the Wald statistic has an approximate χ^2 distribution with one degree of freedom.

More generally, we can test equality of multiple coefficients across quantiles. For example, assuming we have two covariates in addition to the intercept term in the models, we may wish to test whether the conditional pth and qth quantile functions are shifts of one another; that is,

$$H_0: \beta_2^{(p)} = \beta_2^{(q)} \text{ and } \beta_3^{(p)} = \beta_3^{(q)} \text{ versus } H_a: \beta_2^{(p)} \neq \beta_2^{(q)} \text{ or } \beta_3^{(p)} \neq \beta_3^{(q)},$$

with the intercept term left out. A Wald statistic for performing this test can be described as follows. First, we use the estimated covariances to obtain an estimated covariance matrix $\hat{\Sigma}_{\hat{\beta}^{(p)} - \hat{\beta}^{(q)}}$ for $\hat{\beta}^{(p)} - \hat{\beta}^{(q)}$ of the form $\hat{\Sigma}_{\hat{\beta}^{(p)} - \hat{\beta}^{(q)}} = \begin{bmatrix} \hat{\sigma}_{11} & \hat{\sigma}_{12} \\ \hat{\sigma}_{21} & \hat{\sigma}_{22} \end{bmatrix}$, where the entries are obtained by substituting estimated variances and covariances into the following expressions:

$$\sigma_{11} = Var(\hat{\beta}_1^{(p)} - \hat{\beta}_1^{(q)}) = Var(\hat{\beta}_1^{(p)}) + Var(\hat{\beta}_1^{(q)}) - Cov(\hat{\beta}_1^{(p)}, \hat{\beta}_1^{(q)})$$

$$\sigma_{12} = \sigma_{21} = Cov(\hat{\beta}_1^{(p)}, \hat{\beta}_2^{(p)}) + Cov(\hat{\beta}_1^{(q)}, \hat{\beta}_2^{(q)}) - Cov(\hat{\beta}_1^{(p)}, \hat{\beta}_2^{(q)})$$
$$- Cov(\hat{\beta}_1^{(q)}, \hat{\beta}_2^{(p)})$$

$$\sigma_{22} = Var(\hat{\beta}_2^{(p)} - \hat{\beta}_2^{(q)}) = Var(\hat{\beta}_2^{(p)}) + Var(\hat{\beta}_2^{(q)}) - Cov(\hat{\beta}_2^{(p)}, \hat{\beta}_2^{(q)})$$

Next we calculate the test statistic as

$$W = \begin{bmatrix} \hat{\beta}_1^{(p)} - \hat{\beta}_1^{(q)} \\ \hat{\beta}_2^{(p)} - \hat{\beta}_2^{(q)} \end{bmatrix}^t \hat{\Sigma}_{\hat{\beta}^{(p)} - \hat{\beta}^{(q)}}^{-1} \begin{bmatrix} \hat{\beta}_1^{(p)} - \hat{\beta}_1^{(q)} \\ \hat{\beta}_2^{(p)} - \hat{\beta}_2^{(q)} \end{bmatrix},$$

which under the null hypothesis is approximately distributed as χ^2 with two degrees of freedom.

Stata performs the bootstrap procedure for a single QRM using the bsqreg command and for multiple QRMs using the sqreg command. The estimates from the sqreg command are the same as those from the separate estimates using bsqreg, but the sqreg command will provide the entire covariance matrix. The utility of sqreg is that it allows researchers to test for equivalence of coefficients across quantiles. With the advancement of computing technology, the bootstrap method can be used by most researchers. For example, Stata (version 9.2) using a computer with a 64-bit, 1.6-GHz processor takes about eight minutes to complete the estimation of covariances for a two-covariate QRM at the median based on

500 resamples of our income data of over 20,000 households. The corresponding estimation of 19 quantiles with 500 replicates takes two hours.

Goodness of Fit of the QRM

In linear-regression models, the goodness of fit is measured by the R-squared (the coefficient of determination) method:

$$R^2 = \frac{\sum_i (\hat{y}_i - \bar{y})^2}{\sum_i (y_i - \bar{y})^2} = 1 - \frac{\sum_i (y_i - \hat{y})^2}{\sum_i (y_i - \bar{y})^2} \qquad [4.6]$$

The numerator in the second expression is the sum of squared distances between the observed y_i and the corresponding values $\hat{y}_i$ fitted by the model. On the other hand, the denominator is the sum of squared distances between the observed y_i and the fitted values that we would obtain if we included only the intercept term in the model. Thus, we interpret R^2 as the proportion of variation in the dependent variable explained by the predictor variables in the model. This quantity ranges from 0 to 1, with a larger value of R^2 indicating a better model fit.

An analog of the R^2 statistic can be readily developed for quantile-regression models. Since linear-regression-model fits are based on the least-squares criterion and quantile-regression models are based on minimizing a sum of weighted distances $\sum_{i=1}^{n} d_p(y_i, \hat{y}_i)$ as in $(3-5)$—with different weights used depending on whether $y_i > \hat{y}_i$ or $y_i < \hat{y}_i$—we need to measure goodness of fit in a manner that is consistent with this criterion. Koenker and Machado (1999) suggest measuring goodness of fit by comparing the sum of weighted distances for the model of interest with the sum in which only the intercept parameter appears. Let $V^1(p)$ be the sum of weighted distances for the full pth quantile-regression model, and let $V^0(p)$ be the sum of weighted distance for the model that includes only a constant term. For example, using the one-covariate model, we have

$$V^1(p) = \sum_{i=1}^{n} d_p(y_i, \hat{y}_i)$$

$$= \sum_{y_i \geq \beta_0^{(p)} + \beta_1^{(p)} x_i} p|y_i - \beta_0^{(p)} - \beta_1^{(p)} x_i| + \sum_{y_i < \beta_0^{(p)} + \beta_1^{(p)} x_i} (1-p)|y_i - \beta_0^{(p)} - \beta_1^{(p)} x_i|$$

and

$$V^0(p) = \sum_{i=1}^{n} d_p(y_i, \hat{Q}^{(p)}) = \sum_{y_i \geq \bar{y}} p|y_i - \hat{Q}^{(p)}| + \sum_{y_i < \bar{y}} (1 - p)|y_i - \hat{Q}^{(p)}|.$$

For the model that only includes a constant term, the fitted constant is the sample pth quantile $\hat{Q}^{(p)}$ for the sample $y_1, \ldots, y_n$. The goodness of fit is then defined as

$$R(p) = 1 - \frac{V^1(p)}{V^0(p)}. \qquad [4.7]$$

Since the $V^0(p)$ and $V^1(p)$ are nonnegative, $R(p)$ is at most 1. Also, because the sum of weighted distances is minimized for the full-fitted model, $V^1(p)$ is never greater than $V^0(p)$, so $R(p)$ is greater than or equal to zero. Thus, $R(p)$ is within the range of [0, 1], with a larger $R(p)$ indicating a better model fit. Equation 4.7 is a local measure of the goodness of fit of QRM at p. The global assessment of a QRM for the whole distribution requires an examination of the $R(p)$ collectively.

The $R(p)$ defined above allows for comparison of a fitted model with any number of covariates beyond the intercept term to the model in which only the intercept term is present. This is a restricted form of a goodness-of-fit comparison introduced by Koenker and Machado (1999) for nested models. By obvious extension, the improvement in fit for a given model can be measured relative to a more restricted form of the model. The resulting quantity is referred to as the relative $R(p)$ value. Let $V^2(p)$ be the sum of weighted distances for the less restricted pth quantile-regression model, and let $V^1(p)$ be the sum of weighted distance for the more restricted pth quantile-regression model. The relative $R(p)$ can be expressed as:

$$\text{Relative } R(p) = 1 - \frac{V^2(p)}{V^1(p)}. \qquad [4.8]$$

We turn to our income example for illustration. We fit a two-covariate QRM (education and race) and a one-covariate QRM (education only) for income at 19 equispaced quantiles. The values in Table 4.3 represent the measures of goodness of fit for the full model relative to the constant model (see Figure 4.1). Stata provides the measure of goodness of fit using Equation 4.7 and refers to it as "pseudo-R^2" to distinguish it from the ordinary R^2 from LRM.

TABLE 4.3

Goodness of Fit for QRM of Income

Model	0.05	0.10	0.15	0.20	0.25	0.30	0.35	0.40	0.45	0.50	0.55	0.60	0.65	0.70	0.75	0.80	0.85	0.90	0.95	Mean
Two-Covariate Income	.0254	.0441	.0557	.0652	.0726	.0793	.0847	.0897	.0943	.0985	.1025	.1059	.1092	.1120	.1141	.1162	.1179	.1208	.1271	.0913
One-Covariate Income	.0204	.0381	.0496	.0591	.0666	.0732	.0784	.0834	.0881	.0922	.0963	.0998	.1033	.1064	.1092	.1112	.1131	.1169	.1230	.0857

NOTE: The two-covariate model includes education and race and the one-covariate model includes education. The entries are R, the goodness-of-fit measure for the QRM.

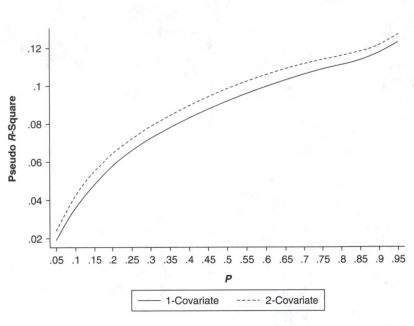

Figure 4.1   Goodness of Fit of QRM: A One-Covariate Model Nested in a Two-Covariate Model

The top panel of Table 4.3 shows the goodness of fit for the two-covariate model. The goodness of fit for income is poorer at the lower tail than the upper tail. The mean $R(p)$ over the 19 quantiles for income is .0913. The one-covariate model is nested in the two-covariate model, with mean $R(p)$ over the 19 quantiles for income being .0857. These models' $R(p)$s indicate that using race as an explanatory variable improves the model fit. As the $R(p)$s for the two-covariate model are only moderately increased in comparison to those for the one-covariate model, however, the major explanatory power lies in education. The formal test of whether adding race significantly improves the model is the t-ratio. The formal test for a group of explanatory variables is beyond the scope of this text. Interested readers can consult Koenker and Machado (1999).

Summary

This chapter discusses inference for quantile-regression models. The asymptotic inference for QRM coefficients (the standard error and the confidence interval) are analogous to the inference of LRM coefficients as long as necessary modifications are made to properly estimate the variance of the error. Given the often-skewed distribution of the dependent variables in social-science studies, the assumptions underlying the asymptotic inference can be questionable and an alternative approach to inference is desirable. The bootstrap method offers an excellent solution. This chapter introduces the bootstrap procedure for QRM coefficients. The idea of bootstrapping is relatively straightforward and, with the advancement of computing technology, quite practical.

In addition, this chapter briefly discusses the goodness of fit of the QRM analogous to that for the LRM. The measure of goodness of fit for the QRM, the $R(p)$, accounts for the appropriate weight each observation takes for a specific quantile equation. The $R(p)$ is easy to comprehend and its interpretation follows the familiar R-squared for the LRM.

Note

1. Recall that the pth quantile of $\varepsilon^{(p)}$ is assumed to be zero in the QRM.

5. INTERPRETATION OF QUANTILE-REGRESSION ESTIMATES

In this chapter, we discuss the interpretation of quantile-regression estimates. We first interpret quantile-regression fits for *specific* quantiles. The median-regression quantile can be used to track location changes. Other specific regression quantiles, for example, the .05th and .95th quantiles, can be used to assess how a covariate predicts the conditional off-central locations as well as shape shifts of the response. We also consider the more general case of sequences of regression quantiles, which can reveal more subtle changes in the shape of the response variable's distribution.

We use the interpretation of LRM estimates as a starting point and interpret the QRM estimates in the context of income inequality. In this way, we demonstrate two key advantages of the QRM approach over LRM: It enables us to model off-central conditional quantiles as well as shape shifts in the distribution of a response variable. Various methods are illustrated using the same income example as in Chapter 3 but now considering education and race simultaneously. Throughout the chapter, we focus on analyses of the raw-scale response. Interpreting estimates for a monotonically transformed response variable and understanding the implications for the raw scale of the response are discussed in Chapter 6.

Reference and Comparison

To facilitate the interpretation of quantile-regression estimates, we use the notions of *reference* and *comparison* as well as some general ideas related to quantification of effects. The reference is a conventional regression term and the comparison is the effect of a unit increase of a covariate in regression.[1]

In many instances, our interest will be on comparing one group to another. For example, we might wish to compare individuals with 11 years of education to those with 12 years of education. Alternatively, we might be interested in comparing blacks to whites. In any case, we start with one possible setting of the covariates, for example, all blacks with 11 years of education, and refer to the subpopulation with these attributes as a *reference* group. Then, we modify one of the covariates in a specific way, for example, changing 11 years to 12 years of education, or change being black to being white. We then refer to the subpopulation corresponding to the changed covariate settings as a *comparison* group. A key feature of these two group comparisons is that a single covariate is modified, leaving the remaining covariates fixed.

Examining how the response distribution is altered when we switch from a reference group to a comparison group helps quantify the *effect* of a change in a single covariate on the distribution of the response. For the LRM, fitted coefficients can be interpreted as estimated effects, that is, estimates of the change in the mean of the response distribution that results from a one-unit increase in a continuous covariate or the change of the value from 0 to 1 of a dummy covariate. Each of these changes can be interpreted as an estimated difference in means between a reference group and a comparison group. The analog for the QRM is an estimated difference in a particular quantile between a reference group and a comparison group, resulting from a one-unit increase in a continuous covariate or the change of the value from 0 to 1 of a dummy covariate, with other covariates held constant.

Conditional Means Versus Conditional Medians

By far, the simplest QRM to understand is the median-regression model (the .5th QRM), which expresses the conditional median of a response variable given predictor variables, and provides a natural alternative to LRM, which fits the conditional mean. These are natural to compare in that they both attempt to model the *central location* of a response-variable distribution.

The income LRM estimate is $6,314 for *ED* and $11,452 for *WHITE*. One more year of schooling is associated with a $6,314 increase in mean income at any fixed level of education. Because of the linearity assumption, the same amount of increase in the conditional mean would occur for households at any fixed level of schooling. For example, one more year of education is associated with a same amount of increase in the mean income for households whose head has 9 or 16 years of schooling. In addition, the effect of an additional year of education is the same for blacks as it is for whites: No interaction between race and education is specified in the model. In terms of reference and comparison groups, we can say that while there are many different reference-group/comparison-group combinations, there are only two possible *effects:* a single race effect and a single education effect.[2]

The LRM includes a rigid assumption: From one group to the next, the income distribution undergoes a shift without an alteration in its scale and shape. In particular, the positive coefficient for education reveals the degree to which the distribution shifts to the right as a result of a one-year change in the level of education, and this is the only way in which distribution change is manifested. Similarly, the coefficient for *WHITE* in the LRM of income on race indicates the rightward location shift from blacks' income distribution to whites' income distribution, again without altering its shape: The mean income of blacks is $11,452 lower than that of whites.

In passing from the LRM to the QRM and focusing on the special case of median regression, the key modification to keep in mind is that we model the conditional *median* rather than the conditional mean. As discussed in Chapter 3, the median might be a more suitable measure of central location for a distribution for a variety of reasons that carry over when we attempt to model the behavior of a collection of conditional distributions. For instance, these conditional distributions might be right-skewed, making their means more a reflection of what is happening in the upper tail of the distributions than a reflection of what is happening in the middle. As a concrete example, families in the top-income percentile may profoundly influence any analysis meant to investigate the effect of education on median income. Consequently, the analysis may reveal education effects for the conditional mean, which is much higher than the conditional median.

The interpretation of a median-regression coefficient is analogous to that of an LRM coefficient. Table 5.1 gives the estimated coefficients for various quantile-regression models, including the median (.5th quantile) regression. In the case of a continuous covariate, the coefficient estimate is interpreted as the change in the median of the response variable corresponding to a unit change in the predictor. The consequences of linearity and no interactions in the LRM apply for the median-regression model. In particular, the effect on the median response of a one-year increase in education is the same for all races and education levels, and the effect of a change in race is the same for all education levels.

TABLE 5.1

Quantile-Regression Estimates and Their Asymptotic Standard Error for Income

	.05	.10	.15	.20	.25	.30	.35	.40	.45	.50	.55	.60	.65	.70	.75	.80	.85	.90	.95
ED	1,130	1,782	2,315	2,757	3,172	3,571	3,900	4,266	4,549	4,794	5,182	5,571	5,841	6,224	6,598	6,954	7,505	8,279	9,575
	(36)	(41)	(51)	(51)	(60)	(61)	(66)	(73)	(82)	(92)	(86)	(102)	(107)	(129)	(154)	(150)	(209)	(316)	(605)
WHITE	3,197	4,689	5,642	6,557	6,724	7,541	8,168	8,744	9,087	9,792	10,475	11,091	11,407	11,739	12,142	12,972	13,249	14,049	17,484
	(359)	(397)	(475)	(455)	(527)	(528)	(561)	(600)	(662)	(727)	(664)	(776)	(793)	(926)	(1,065)	(988)	(1,299)	(1,790)	(2,895)

NOTE: Asymptotic standard errors are in parentheses.

The coefficient for *ED* in the conditional-median model is $4,794, which is lower than the coefficient in the conditional-mean model. This suggests that while an increase of one year of education gives rise to an average increase of $6,314 in income, the increase would not be as substantial for most of the population. Similarly, the coefficient for *WHITE* in the conditional-median model is $9,792, lower than the corresponding coefficient in the conditional-mean model.

The asymptotic standard errors of estimates under the assumption of i.i.d. are shown in parentheses. If the i.i.d. assumption holds, the standard error of the education effect on the median of income is $92, the *t*-ratio is 52.1, and the *p*-value is less than .001, providing evidence to reject the null hypothesis that education has no effect on the median income. The coefficient for *WHITE* has a standard error of $727 and is statistically significant at the .001 level.

Interpretation of Other Individual Conditional Quantiles

Sometimes, researchers are more interested in the lower or upper tails of a distribution than in the central location. Education policy concerning equality focuses on elevating the test scores of underachieving students. In 2000, 39% of 8th graders were below the basic achievement level of science. Thus, the .39th quantile is more relevant than the mean or median for educational researchers. Welfare policy targets the lower-income population. If the national poverty rate is 11%, the .11th income quantile and quantiles below that level become more relevant than the median or the mean for welfare researchers. Researchers find that union membership yields a greater return at the lower end of the income distribution than at the mean (Chamberlain, 1994). On the other hand, for the top 10% of income earners in the population, education at prestigious private universities tends to be more common. Studies of the benefits of prestigious higher education may focus on the 90th income quantile and above.

The coefficients of QRM fits for 19 quantiles in Table 5.1 can be used to examine effects of education and race on various income quantiles.[3] To inform welfare policymakers, we examine the education and race coefficients at the .10th and .05th quantiles of the conditional-income models. We see that one more year of education can increase income by $1,782 at the .10th quantile and $1,130 at the .05th quantile, and the black-white gap is $4,689 at the .10th quantile and $3,197 at the .05th quantile. For researchers interested in return to education at the right tail, we look at the estimates of education at the .90th and .95th quantiles. The coefficient for the .95th quantile is $9,575, much larger than that at the .90th quantile ($8,279), suggesting the contribution of prestigious higher education to income disparity. Under the i.i.d. assumption, the asymptotic standard errors indicate that the education effect and the racial effect are significant at the off-central quantiles as well.

Because the i.i.d. is a very restrictive assumption that assumes no shape shift of the response, more flexible approaches to estimation of standard errors, such as bootstrapping, should be used. Table 5.2 presents the point estimate and standard error of parameters for the two covariates based on a 500-resample bootstrap procedure. The bootstrapped point estimates are similar to the asymptotic estimates, but they tend to vary to a lesser degree across quantiles than do the asymptotic standard errors, particularly for *ED* (see Figures 5.1 and 5.2).

Tests for Equivalence of Coefficients Across Quantiles

When multiple quantile regressions are estimated, we need to test whether apparent differences are statistically significant. To perform such a test, the covariance matrix of cross-quantile estimates must be estimated. This covariance matrix is estimated numerically via bootstrapping to allow flexible errors and provide a numerical solution to the very complex asymptotic formulae.

Table 5.3 presents the point estimates, bootstrap standard errors, and p-values for tests of equivalence of the estimates at the pth quantile against those at the median, those at the $(1 - p)$th quantile, and those at the $(p + .05)$th quantile for $p \leq .5$. Depending on the circumstances, the bootstrap method can give smaller or larger standard errors than using asymptotic methods. For example, at the median income, the asymptotic method gives a point estimate of \$4,794 and a standard error of \$92 for education. The corresponding numbers using bootstrap are \$4,794 and \$103. However, at the .05th quantile, the bootstrap reports a lower level of precision of the estimate for education than the asymptotic method: The bootstrap standard error is \$80, larger than the asymptotic standard error (\$36).

The p-values for Wald tests of equivalence of estimates across quantiles show that the effect of education differs across quantiles in all of our selected tests. These tests compare the current estimate (say, at the .05th quantile) against three estimates: those at the median, those at the corresponding position in the opposite tail (at the .95th quantile), and those at the adjacent higher quantile (at the .10th quantile). In contrast, the race effect does not statistically differ in a substantial number of our selected tests. For example, the white effect at the .20th quantile is not significantly different from that at the .25th quantile. In particular, the race effect on income quantiles above the median does not differ statistically from the corresponding effect on the

TABLE 5.2

Point Estimate and Standard Error of

Quantile-Regression Estimate for Income: 500-Resample Bootstrap

	.05	.10	.15	.20	.25	.30	.35	.40	.45	.50	.55	.60	.65	.70	.75	.80	.85	.90	.95
ED	1,130	1,782	2,315	2,757	3,172	3,571	3,900	4,266	4,549	4,794	5,182	5,571	5,841	6,224	6,598	6,954	7,505	8,279	9,575
	(80)	(89)	(81)	(56)	(149)	(132)	(76)	(98)	(90)	(103)	(83)	(103)	(121)	(125)	(154)	(151)	(141)	(216)	(268)
WHITE	3,197	4,689	5,642	6,557	6,724	7,541	8,168	8,744	9,087	9,792	10,475	11,091	11,407	11,739	12,142	12,972	13,249	14,049	17,484
	(265)	(319)	(369)	(380)	(469)	(778)	(477)	(545)	(577)	(624)	(589)	(715)	(803)	(769)	(1,041)	(929)	(1,350)	(1,753)	(2,280)

NOTE: Bootstrap standard errors are in parentheses.

61

TABLE 5.3

Equivalence of Coefficients Across

Quantiles of Income: 500-Resample Bootstrap

			P-Value		
Quantile/ Variable	Coefficient	Different From Coeff. at Median?	Different From Coeff. at (1 − p)th Quantile?	Different From Coeff. at (p + .05)th Quantile?	4 Coeff. Jointly Different?
.05th Quantile					
ED	1130** (80)	0.0000	0.0000	0.0000	0.0000
WHITE	3197** (265)	0.0000	0.0000	0.0000	0.0000
.10th Quantile					
ED	1782** (89)	0.0000	0.0000	0.0000	0.0000
WHITE	4689** (319)	0.0000	0.0000	0.0000	0.0000
.15th Quantile					
ED	2315** (81)	0.0000	0.0000	0.0000	0.0000
WHITE	5642** (369)	0.0000	0.0000	0.0018	0.0000
.20th Quantile					
ED	2757** (56)	0.0000	0.0000	0.0000	0.0000
WHITE	6557** (380)	0.0000	0.0000	0.4784	0.0000
.25th Quantile					
ED	3172** (149)	0.0000	0.0000	0.0000	0.0000
WHITE	6724** (469)	0.0000	0.0000	0.0012	0.0000
.30th Quantile					
ED	3571** (132)	0.0000	0.0000	0.0000	0.0000
WHITE	7541** (778)	0.0000	0.0000	0.0142	0.0000
.35th Quantile					
ED	3900** (76)	0.0000	0.0000	0.0000	0.0000
WHITE	8168** (477)	0.0000	0.0000	0.0035	0.0000

Quantile/ Variable	Coefficient	P-Value			
		Different From Coeff. at Median?	Different From Coeff. at $(1-p)$th Quantile?	Different From Coeff. at $(p+.05)$th Quantile?	4 Coeff. Jointly Different?
.40th Quantile					
ED	4266** (98)	0.0000	0.0000	0.0000	0.0000
WHITE	8744** (545)	0.0028	0.0008	0.1034	0.0002
.45th Quantile					
ED	4549** (90)	0.0000	0.0000	0.0000	—
WHITE	9087** (577)	0.0243	0.0017	0.0243	—
.50th Quantile					
ED	4794** (103)	—	—	0.0000	—
WHITE	9792** (624)	—	—	0.0361	—

NOTE: Standard errors are in parentheses.

$**p < .01$

adjacent $p+.05$ quantiles, as opposed to the effect of education, which becomes stronger as p increases.

One can also test the null hypothesis that more than two quantile coefficients for the same covariate are jointly the same. The last column of Table 5.3 shows the results for the joint test of four quantile coefficients for the same covariate. The Wald test statistics have an approximate χ^2 distribution with three degrees of freedom. The tests lead to the rejection of the null hypothesis and the conclusion that at least two of the four coefficients are significantly different from each other.[4]

Using the QRM Results to Interpret Shape Shifts

Much social-science research, particularly inequality research, needs to account not only for location shifts but for shape shifts, because, to a great extent, focusing on location alone ignores a substantial amount of information about group differences. Two of the most important shape features to consider are scale (or spread) and skewness.

A Graphical View

Because we are interested in how predictor variables change the shape of the response distribution, we use the QRM to produce estimates at multiple quantiles. The analysis of shape effects can be considerably more complex than the analysis of location, and we see an important trade-off. On the one hand, shape analysis, which can be carried out by making use of multiple sets of QRM estimates at various quantiles, has the potential to reveal more information than the analysis of location effects alone. On the other hand, describing this additional information can be cumbersome and requires additional effort. In particular, examination of quantile-regression coefficients for a long sequence of quantile values (for example, .05, .10, . . . , .90, .95) is unwieldy, and a graphical view of QRM estimates becomes a necessary step in interpreting QRM results.

The QRM coefficients for a particular covariate reveal the effect of a unit change in the covariate on quantiles of the response distribution. Consequently, arrays of these coefficients for a range of quantiles can be used to determine how a one-unit increase in the covariate affects the shape of the response distribution. We highlight this shape-shift effect by a graphical view examining coefficients. For a particular covariate, we plot the coefficients and the confidence envelope, where the predictor variable effect $\hat{\beta}^{(p)}$ is on the y-axis and the value of p is on the x-axis.

Figure 5.1 provides a graphical view for the income quantiles as a function of education and race (both centered at their respective means). Using the estimated coefficients (see Table 5.1), we draw a graph of the effect of *ED* (*WHITE*) and the 95% confidence envelope. We also draw the graph for the fitted *CONSTANT*. Because the covariates have been centered about their means, *CONSTANT* gives the fitted quantile function at the covariate mean, which is referred to as the *typical setting*. This conditional-quantile function at the typical setting is right-skewed given the flat slopes below the median and the steep slopes above the median.

The effect of *ED* can be described as the change in a conditional-income quantile brought about by one additional year of education, at any level of education, fixing race. The education effect is significantly positive, because the confidence envelope does not cross the zero line (see the thick horizontal line). Figure 5.1a shows an upward-sloping curve for the effects of education: The effect of one more year of schooling is positive for all values of p and steadily increasing with p. This increase accelerates after the .80th quantile.

The effect of *WHITE* can be described as the change in the conditional-income quantile brought about by changing the race from black to white,

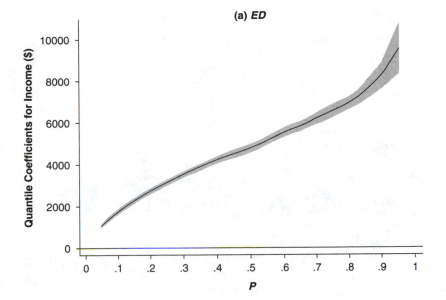

(a) *ED*

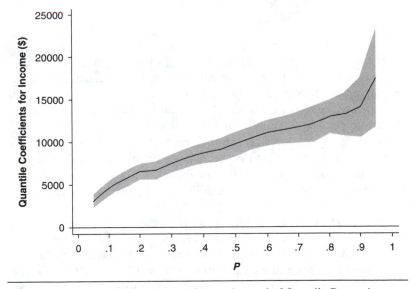

(b) *WHITE*

Figure 5.1   Asymptotic 95% Confidence Interval of Quantile-Regression
Estimates: Income

(Continued)

(c) Constant ("Typical Setting")

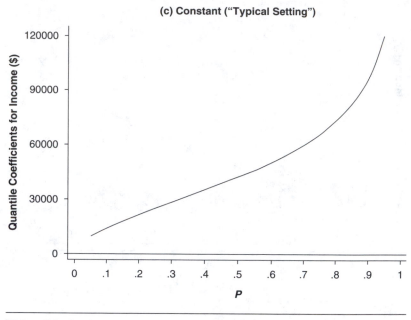

Figure 5.1 (Continued)

fixing the education level. The effect of being white is significantly positive, as the zero line is far below the confidence envelope. Figure 5.1b depicts another upward-sloping curve for the effect of being white as compared with being black. The slopes below the .15th quantile and above the .90th quantile are steeper than those at the middle quantiles.

Figure 5.2 is the graph corresponding to Figure 5.1 except that the confidence envelope is based on bootstrap estimates. We observe that the bootstrapping confidence envelope in Figure 5.2 is more balanced than the asymptotic confidence envelope in Figure 5.1. We draw a similar shape-shift pattern from Figures 5.1 and 5.2.

These graphs convey additional patterns related to the effects of education and race. First, education and race are responsible for location shifts as well as shape shifts. If there were only location shifts, increasing education by a single year or changing race from black to white would cause every quantile to increase by the same amount, leading to a graph of $\hat{\beta}^{(p)}$ versus p resembling a horizontal line. Instead, we see that $\hat{\beta}^{(p)}$ is monotonically

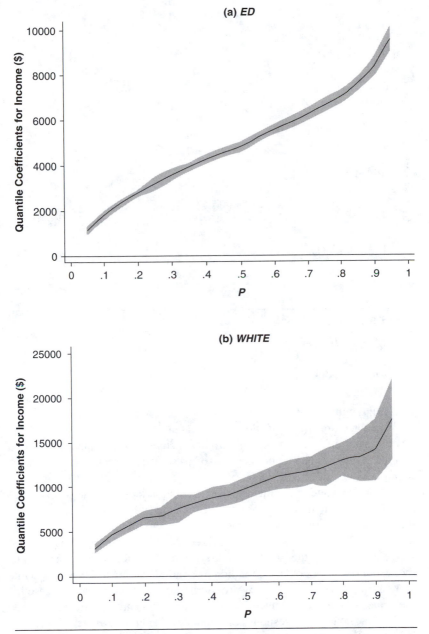

Figure 5.2 Bootstrap 95% Confidence Interval of Quantile-Regression Estimates: Income

(Continued)

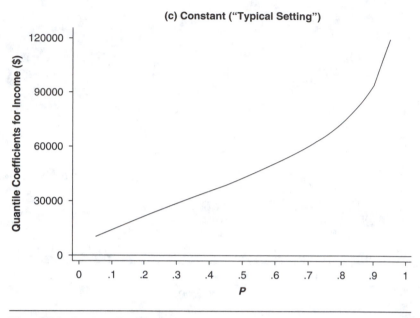

Figure 5.2 (Continued)

increasing with p, that is, $\hat{\beta}^{(p)} > \hat{\beta}^{(q)}$ whenever $p > q$, and this property tells us that an additional year of education or changing race from black to white has a greater effect on income for higher-income brackets than for lower-income brackets. The monotonicity also has scale-effect implications, since it implies that $\hat{\beta}^{(1-p)} - \hat{\beta}^{(p)} > 0$ for $p < .5$. In other words, changing race from black to white or adding a year of education increases the scale of the response.[5] Although both graphs appear to suggest changes more complex than location and scale, the graphical view is not sufficient to reveal skewness shifts, because skewness is measured using multiple quantiles.

We now sum up the graphical patterns for the effect of a covariate on the response. A horizontal line indicates a pure location shift by a one-unit increase in the covariate; an upward-sloping curve indicates an increase in the scale, whereas a downward-sloping curve indicates a decrease in the scale of the conditional-response distribution. The graphical view, however, is not sufficient to demonstrate the skewness shift. The graphical view provides some indication of how modifications of the predictor variables produce shape shifts. We are also interested in how large the shift is and whether the shift is significant. Our next task is to develop quantitative measures for two types of shape shifts from the QRM estimates.

Scale Shifts

The standard deviation is a commonly employed measure of the scale or spread for a symmetric distribution. For skewed distributions, however, distances between selected quantiles provide a more informed description of the spread than the standard deviation. For a value of p between 0 and .5, we identify two sample quantiles: $\hat{Q}^{(1-p)}$ (the $[1-p]$th quantile) and $\hat{Q}^{(p)}$ (the pth quantile). The pth interquantile range, $IQR^{(p)} = \hat{Q}^{(1-p)} - \hat{Q}^{(p)}$, is a measure of spread. This quantity describes the range of the middle $(1 - 2p)$ proportion of the distribution. When $p = .25$, the interquantile range becomes the interquartile range $IQR^{(.25)} = Q^{(.75)} - Q^{(.25)}$, giving the range of the middle 50% of the distribution. Other values of p, for example, .10, .05, .025, can be used as well to capture spread further out in two tails of a distribution. For example, using $p = .10$, the pth interquantile range gives the range of the middle 80% of the distribution.

Figure 5.3 compares a *reference* group and a *comparison* group, which have the same median M. Fixing some choice of p, we can measure an interquantile range $IQR_R = U_R - L_R$ for the reference group, and $IQR_C = U_C - L_C$ for the comparison group. We then use the *difference-in-differences* $IQR_C - IQR_R$ as a measure of scale shift. In the figure, the comparison group's scale is larger than that of the reference group, which results in a positive scale shift.

Turning to our application example, Table 5.4 shows the scale changes of the household income distribution for different educational groups using two methods; one approach uses *sample quantiles,* that is, quantiles calculated directly from the two group samples, and the second approach makes use of fitted coefficients for covariates from the income QRM. The sample quantiles lead to an interquartile range of $26,426 for the group with 11 years of schooling and $34,426 for the group with twelve years of schooling. The sample spread for the 12-year-education group is $8,000 higher than for the 11-year-education group. This scale shift can be obtained by computing the difference between the interquartile ranges $Q^{(.75)} - Q^{(.25)}$ for the two groups. We see that from 11 to 12 years, the interquartile range increased by $34,426 - 26,426 = $8,000$. Using the same approach for other interquantile ranges, we find that the scale increase is $15,422 for the middle 80% of the sample, $19,736 for the middle 90%, and $28,052 for the middle 95%.

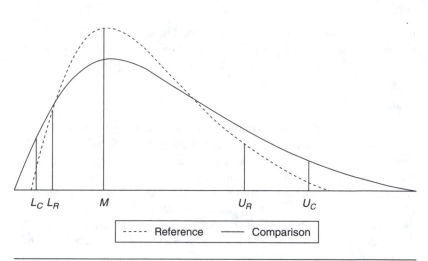

Figure 5.3   Scale Shifts

The QRM fits provide an alternative approach to estimating scale-shift effects. Here, we use the notation $\hat{\beta}^{(p)}$ to refer to the fitted coefficient corresponding to some covariate in a pth quantile-regression model. Such a coefficient indicates the increase or decrease in any particular quantile brought about by a unit increase in the covariate. Thus, when we increase the covariate by one unit, the corresponding pth interquantile range changes by the amount $\hat{\beta}^{(1-p)} - \hat{\beta}^{(p)}$, which is the pth scale-shift effect denoted by $SCS^{(p)}$.

$$
\begin{aligned}
SCS^{(p)} = IQR_C^{(p)} - IQR_R^{(p)} &= (Q_C^{(1-p)} - Q_C^{(p)}) - (Q_R^{(1-p)} - Q_R^{(p)}) \\
&= (Q_C^{(1-p)} - Q_R^{(1-p)}) - (Q_C^{(p)} - Q_R^{(p)}) \\
&= \hat{\beta}^{(1-p)} - \hat{\beta}^{(p)} \text{ for } p < .5.
\end{aligned}
\qquad [5.1]
$$

If we fit a linear QRM with no interaction terms between covariates, the scale effect does not depend on the particular covariate setting (the reference group). When $SCS^{(p)}$ is zero, there is apparently no evidence of scale change. A negative value indicates that increasing the covariate results in a decrease in scale, while a positive value indicates the opposite effect.

Using Equation 5.1 and estimates from Table 5.2, the scale shift brought about by one more year of schooling for the middle 50% of the population is $3,426 (subtracting the coefficient at the .25th quantile from that at the .75th quantile: $6,598 – $3,172 = $3,426). There are two reasons why this scale shift is smaller than the observed scale shift of $8,000. The model-based measure is a partial measure, controlling for other covariates (here, race). Also, the scale shift based on sample quantiles is specific for two education groups, whereas the model-based measure considers all education groups. With Equation 5.1, we interpret the QRM coefficients for education as increases in scale by \$6,497 for the middle 80% of the population, \$8,445 for the middle 90% of the population, and \$10,902 for the middle 95% of the population (see the last column of Table 5.4).

We can interpret the racial effect in terms of scale shifts in the same fashion. Using Table 5.2, controlling for education, whites' income spread is higher than blacks' income spread: \$12,142 − \$6,724 = \$5,418 for the middle 50% of the population, \$14,049 − \$4,689 = \$9,360 for the middle 80%, and \$17,484 − \$3,197 = \$14,287 for the middle 90%.

A scale change can proportionally stretch or contract the segments above and below the median, while keeping the original skewness intact. It can also disproportionately stretch or contract the segments above and below the median, while changing the skewness. Equation 5.1 is unable to distinguish between proportional and disproportional scale shifts.

TABLE 5.4

Scale Shifts of Income Distribution
From 11-Year to 12-Year Education

| Quantile and Quantile Range | Sample-Based | | | Model-Based |
	Education = 11 (1)	Education = 12 (2)	Difference (2) − (1)	
$Q_{.025}$	3387	5229	1842	665
$Q_{.05}$	5352	7195	1843	1130
$Q_{.10}$	6792	10460	3668	1782
$Q_{.25}$	12098	18694	6596	3172
$Q_{.75}$	38524	53120	14596	6598
$Q_{.90}$	58332	77422	19090	8279
$Q_{.95}$	74225	95804	21579	9575
$Q_{.975}$	87996	117890	29894	11567
$Q_{.75} - Q_{.25}$	26426	34426	8000	
$\hat{\beta}^*_{.75} - \hat{\beta}^*_{.25}$				3426
$Q_{.90} - Q_{.10}$	51540	66962	15422	
$\hat{\beta}^*_{.90} - \hat{\beta}^*_{.10}$				6497
$Q_{.95} - Q_{.05}$	68873	88609	19736	
$\hat{\beta}^*_{.95} - \hat{\beta}^*_{.05}$				8445
$Q_{.975} - Q_{.025}$	84609	112661	28052	
$\hat{\beta}^*_{.975} - \hat{\beta}^*_{.025}$				10902

Skewness Shifts

A disproportional scale shift that relates to greater skewness indicates an additional effect on the shape of the response distribution. Chapter 2 developed a direct measure of quantile-based skewness, QSK, defined as the ratio of the upper spread to the lower spread minus 1 (recall Equation 2.2). If QSK is greater than 0, the distribution is right-skewed, and vice versa. Recall Figure 3.2, where the box graphs for education groups and racial groups show this imbalance of upper and lower spreads. Columns 1 and 2 of the middle panel (quantile range) in Table 5.5 present the upper and lower spreads for two education groups with 11 and 12 years of schooling, respectively. We can see that both groups have a right-skewed income distribution for the middle 50%, 80%, 90%, and 95% of the sample.

When we examine whether the skewness of a comparison group differs from that of a reference group, we look for disproportional scale shifts. Figure 5.4 illustrates such a disproportional scale shift for right-skewed distributions in a hypothetical situation. Let M_R and M_C indicate the median of the reference and the comparison, respectively. The upper spread is $U_R - M_R$ for the reference and $U_C - M_C$ for the comparison. The lower spread is $M_R - L_R$ for the reference and $M_C - L_C$ for the comparison. The disproportion can be measured by taking the ratio of $(U_C - M_C)/(U_R - M_R)$ to $(M_C - L_C)/(M_R - L_R)$. If this "ratio-of-ratios" equals 1, then there is no skewness shift. If the ratio-of-ratios is less than 1, the right-skewness is reduced. If the ratio-of-ratios is greater than 1, the right-skewness is increased. The shift in terms of percentage change can be obtained by this quantity minus 1. We call this quantity *skewness shift*, or *SKS*.

Let's look at the sample-based *SKS* in Table 5.5, the skewness shift of the group with 12 years of schooling from the group with 11 years of schooling. Although we learned from the last section that the scale of the more-educated group is larger than that of the less-educated group, the right-skewness is considerably lower in the more-educated group, as the *SKS* is $-.282$ for the middle 50% of the sample, $-.248$ for the middle 80%, $-.283$ for the middle 95%, and $-.195$ for the middle 95%. The skewness reduction is between -19.5% and -28.3% over a variety of quantile ranges.

Our task is to use the QRM coefficients to obtain model-based *SKS*, which involves the conditional quantiles of the reference group. We specify the typical covariate setting as the reference (the estimated constant $\hat{\alpha}$). The *SKS* for the middle $100(1 - 2p)\%$ of the population is:

$$SKS^{(p)} = [(Q_C^{(1-p)} - Q_C^{(.5)})/(Q_R^{(1-p)} - Q_R^{(.5)})]/[(Q_C^{(.5)} - Q_C^{(p)})/(Q_R^{(.5)} - Q_R^{(p)})] - 1$$

$$= [(\hat{\beta}^{(1-p)} + \hat{\alpha}^{(1-p)} - \hat{\beta}^{(.5)} - \hat{\alpha}^{(.5)})/(\hat{\alpha}^{(1-p)} - \hat{\alpha}^{(.5)})]/$$
$$[(\hat{\beta}^{(.5)} + \hat{\alpha}^{(.5)} - \hat{\beta}^{(p)} - \hat{\alpha}^{(p)})/(\hat{\alpha}^{(.5)} - \hat{\alpha}^{(p)})] - 1. \qquad [5.2]$$

TABLE 5.5

Skewness Shifts of Income

Distribution Due to One More Year of Schooling

	Sample-Based			Model-Based		
p	Quantile $(ED = 11)$	Quantile $(ED = 12)$	$SKS^{(p)}$	QRM $\hat{\beta}$	QRM $\hat{\alpha}$	$SKS^{(p)}$
.025	3387	5229	−.195	665	6900	−.049
.05	5352	7195	−.283	1130	9850	−.047
.10	6792	10460	−.248	1782	14168	−.037
.25	12098	18694	−.282	3172	24932	−.016
.50	20985	32943		4794	42176	
.75	38524	53120		6598	65745	
.90	58332	77422		8279	94496	
.95	74225	95804		9575	120104	
.975	87996	117890		11567	150463	
Quantile Range						
$Q_{.75} - Q_{.50}$	17539	20177				
$Q_{.50} - Q_{.25}$	8887	14249				
$Q_{.90} - Q_{.50}$	37347	44479				
$Q_{.50} - Q_{.10}$	14193	22483				
$Q_{.95} - Q_{.50}$	53240	62861				
$Q_{.50} - Q_{.05}$	15633	25748				
$Q_{.975} - Q_{.50}$	67011	84947				
$Q_{.50} - Q_{.025}$	17598	27714				

NOTE: The sample-based $SKS^{(p)} = [(Q_C^{(1-p)} - Q_C^{(.5)})/(Q_R^{(1-p)} - Q_R^{(.5)})]/[(Q_C^{(.5)} - Q_C^{(p)})/(Q_R^{(.5)} - Q_R^{(p)})] - 1$.

For the middle 50% population, we have:

$$SKS^{(.25)} = [(Q_C^{(.75)} - Q_C^{(.5)})/(Q_R^{(.75)} - Q_R^{(.5)})]/[(Q_C^{(.5)} - Q_C^{(.25)})/(Q_R^{(.5)} - Q_R^{(.25)})] - 1$$

$$= [20177/17539]/[14249/8887] - 1$$

$$= [1.150/1.603]$$

$$= -.283$$

The model-based skewness shift is

$$SKS^{(p)} = [(\hat{\beta}^{(1-p)} - \hat{\alpha}^{(1-p)} - \hat{\beta}^{(.5)} - \hat{\alpha}^{(.5)})/(\hat{\alpha}^{(1-p)} - \hat{\alpha}^{(.5)})]/[(\hat{\beta}^{(.5)} + \hat{\alpha}^{(.5)} - \hat{\beta}^{(p)} - \hat{\alpha}^{(p)})/(\hat{\alpha}^{(.5)} - \hat{\alpha}^{(p)})] - 1$$

For the middle 50% population, we have:

$$SKS^{(.25)} = [(\hat{\beta}^{(.75)} + \hat{\alpha}^{(.75)} - \hat{\beta}^{(.5)} - \hat{\alpha}^{(.5)})/(\hat{\alpha}^{(.75)} - \hat{\alpha}^{(.5)})]/[(\hat{\beta}^{(.5)} + \hat{\alpha}^{(.5)} - \hat{\beta}^{(.25)} - \hat{\alpha}^{(.25)})/(\hat{\alpha}^{(.5)} - \hat{\alpha}^{(.25)})] - 1$$

$$= [(6598 + 65745 - 4794 - 42176)/(65745 - 42176)]/$$
$$[(4794 + 42176 - 3172 - 24932)/(42176 - 24932)] - 1$$

$$= [25373/23569]/[18866/17244]$$

$$= [1.077/1.094]$$

$$= -.016$$

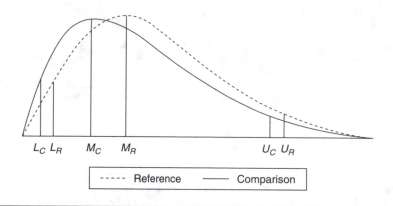

$L_C \; L_R$ M_C M_R $U_C \; U_R$

----- Reference   ——— Comparison

Figure 5.4   Skewness Shifts

Note that because we take the ratio of two ratios, *SKS* effectively elimi-nates the influence of a proportional scale shift. When $SKS = 0$, it indicates either no scale shift or a proportional scale shift. Thus, *SKS* is a measure of skewness above and beyond proportional scale shifts. $SKS < 0$ indicates a reduction of right-skewness due to the effect of the explanatory variable whereas $SKS > 0$ indicates an exacerbation of right-skewness.

The right panel (the model-based panel) of Table 5.5 presents the estimated coefficient for education ($\hat{\beta}$), the estimated constant for the typical covariate setting ($\hat{\alpha}$), and the model-based *SKS*. One more year of schooling slightly decreases right-skewness for all four selected *SKS*s. The percentage decreases range from −1.6% to −4.9%. These model-based estimates are much smaller than the sample-based *SKS*, because the model-based partial effect of educa-tion is a shift from the typical covariate setting, controlling for race.

The impact of being white is a less-skewed conditional income (see Table 5.6): −6.6% for the middle 50% of the population, −8.5% for the mid-dle 80% of the population, −8.7% for the middle 90% of the population, and −7.6% for the middle 95% of the population. It appears that the reduc-tion is greater for the middle 80% and 90% of the population than for the middle 50% of the population. This finding indicates a greater expansion of the white upper middle class than the black upper middle class.

We have developed an overall evaluation of a covariate's impact on the inequality of the response, which examines the alignment of the signs of loca-tion, scale, and skewness shifts when these shifts are statistically significant. A positive, significant location shift indicates that the comparison group's median is higher than that of the reference group. A positive, significant scale shift indicates the comparison group's spread is greater than that of the reference group. Furthermore, a positive, significant skewness shift indicates

TABLE 5.6

Skewness Shifts of Income

Distribution From Black to White: Model-Based

P	QRM $\hat{\beta}$	QRM $\hat{\alpha}$	SKS$^{(p)}$
.025	2576	6900	–0.076
.05	3197	9850	–0.087
.10	4689	14168	–0.085
.25	6724	24932	–0.066
.50	9792	42176	
.75	12142	65745	
.90	14049	94496	
.95	17484	120104	
.975	22092	150463	

that the comparison group is more right-skewed than the reference group. If we reverse-code the reference as the comparison and the comparison as the reference, we have three negative shifts. Thus, the sign alignment of shifts, which we call *in-sync* shifts, makes the total distribution more unequal and the disadvantaged more concentrated. When the three shifts induced by a predictor are in sync, this predictor exacerbates inequality through both location and shape changes. Inconsistent signs of shifts indicate that the predictor variable changes the location and shape of the response in an opposite direction, and the predictor's total effect on the response inequality is compromised. We refer to this pattern as *out of sync*.

Table 5.7 summarizes this overall evaluation for our income example. Bootstrap confidence intervals are also presented. If the confidence interval bounds include zero, at the 95% significance level, we are not certain whether the shift is positive or negative. Only one shift statistic is insignificant in Table 5.7 (the *SKS* of *WHITE* for the middle 50% of the population).

Table 5.7 shows that one more year of education induces a positive location and scale shift but a negative skewness shift. The pattern is out of sync. Similarly, being white induces a positive location and scale shift with a negative skewness shift, exhibiting an out-of-sync pattern. Therefore, our simple model suggests that while higher education and being white are associated with a higher median income and a wider income spread, the income distributions for the less educated and for blacks are more skewed. If this simple model is correct, neither education nor race exacerbates income inequality. This example demonstrates the value of categorizing variables as having in-sync or out-of-sync effects in summarizing many estimates from the QRM. Once we determine a variable's effect regarding sync, as for education or race above, we can easily determine whether or not it makes a contribution to inequality.

TABLE 5.7

Point Estimate and 95% Confidence

Interval of Shape Shifts: 500-Resample Bootstrap

Variable	Location (.50)	SCS (.025 to .975)	SKS (.025 to .975)	SKS (.05 to .95)	SKS (.10 to .90)	SKS (.25 to .75)
Income						
ED	4794	10920	−.049	−.046	−.037	−.017
Lower bound	4592	10162	−.056	−.053	−.044	−.028
Upper bound	4966	11794	−.041	−.038	−.029	−.005
WHITE	9792	19027	−.079	−.090	−.088	−.067
Lower bound	9474	10602	−.151	−.147	−.152	−.136
Upper bound	10110	26712	−.023	−.037	−.024	.005

Summary

This chapter develops various ways to interpret estimates from the quantile-regression model (QRM). Beyond the traditional examination of covariates' effects on specific conditional quantiles, such as the median or positions at the lower or upper quantiles, we expand to the distributional interpretation. We illustrate graphical interpretations of QRM estimates and quantitative measures of shape changes from QRM estimates, including location shifts, scale shifts, and skewness shifts. Our household income example illustrates the direct utility of the QRM estimates in analyzing the contribution of covariates on income inequality.

This chapter focuses on interpretations of the QRM based on raw-scale response variables. These interpretations are directly applied to linearly transformed response variables. However, for a better model fit, skewed response variables are often transformed monotonically. For example, log transformation is the most popular one for right-skewed distributions. Estimates of effects have differing interpretations depending on whether the response variable is represented on a raw scale or on a log scale. In addition, the choice of a modeling approach is important in that the conclusions reached from the analysis of one model may not have valid analogs for the other. For this reason, we devote Chapter 6 to the specific issues arising from monotone transformation of the response variable.

Notes

1. The reference/comparison terminology is used in Handcock and Morris (1999).

2. One can speak of the effect of an additional year of education, and this will be the same for all races and for all education levels. Similarly, there is an effect of switching from being black to being white, which is the same for all education levels. There is also a white-to-black effect, which is opposite of the black-to-white effect. The analysis of location effects for LRM with no interactions is quite simple. The analysis becomes considerably more complicated when we introduce interactions into the model.

3. Note that we can specify any quantiles, such as the .39th quantile, rather than equal-distance quantiles.

4. There are many different and potentially less conservative approaches to multiple testing than the one presented here. For example, a form of studentized range test (Scheffé, 1959) can be used.

5. The effect on scale of a unit change in the covariate is given by

$$SCALE(y|x+1) - SCALE(y|x) =$$

$$[(Q^{(1-p)}(y|x+1) - Q^{(p)}(y|x+1)] - [(Q^{(1-p)}(y|x) - Q^{(p)}(y|x)] =$$

$$[(\hat{\beta}^{(1-p)}(x+1) - (\hat{\beta}^{(p)}(x+1))] - [(\hat{\beta}^{(1-p)}x - \hat{\beta}^{(p)}x)] = \beta^{(1-p)} - \beta^{(p)} \text{ for } p < .5.$$

6. INTERPRETATION OF
MONOTONE-TRANSFORMED QRM

When fitting regression models, it is usually appropriate to apply a log transformation to right-skewed response variables in order to ensure that the model assumptions are at least close to being satisfied. Log transformations are also practical, since they allow interpretation of predictor variable effects in relative terms. Similarly, taking the square (or some other power greater than one) of left-skewed response variables can make the new distribution more symmetric. These nonlinear, *monotonic* transformations, while capable of improving the model fit, no longer preserve the original distribution. When modeling location and shape shifts associated with a change in a particular covariate, it makes much more sense to analyze these shifts on a raw scale than on the monotonically transformed scale. Thus, to aid a substantively sensible interpretation of QRM for monotonically transformed response variables, we need to obtain effects of covariates on the raw scale from transformed-scale coefficients. This chapter uses the log-transformation case to discuss two methods that fulfill the goal. These methods can be applied to any monotone transformation of the response variable.

Location Shifts on the Log Scale

We start from location shifts. One way to model the central location of the response variable is to consider the conditional-mean model relating education to log income. Table 6.1 shows that each additional year of education increases the conditional-mean income by a factor of $e^{.128} = 1.137$, which indicates a 13.7% increase.[1] The corresponding fitted-median model in Table 6.2 (middle column $p = .5$) gives a coefficient of .131, which indicates that one more year of education increases the conditional-median income by $e^{.131} = 1.140$, or 14.0%. In relative terms, the education effect has a slightly stronger effect on the conditional median, whereas in absolute terms, the education effect is stronger on the conditional mean, as shown in Chapter 5.

Because the concept of a percent increase requires the specification of a *reference* group, when a predictor variable is categorical, that is, indicating group membership, some care has to be taken to choose an appropriate reference category to facilitate interpretation. For example, suppose we fit a model in which log income is expressed as a function of race (*BLACK/WHITE*), using 0 to indicate black and 1 to indicate white. Our fitted LRM (Table 6.1) says that the coefficient is .332, indicating that whites' income is greater than blacks' by a factor of $e^{.332} = 1.393$, a 39.3% increase in income. On the other hand, if we adopt the reverse code, using 0 to indicate white and 1 to indicate black, the linear equivariance property of the LRM tells us that the coefficient for *BLACK* should be −.332. Here the interpretation of the negative coefficient for *BLACK* does not correspond to a 39.3% *decrease* in income. Instead, the factor would be $e^{-.332} = 0.717$, that is, a 28.3% decrease in income. This point becomes clearer for larger values of the coefficient. For example, a coefficient of 2 in the first model would indicate that whites experience an increase of income of 639% over that of blacks, but in the second model, the coefficient would be −2, and this would correspond to blacks' income being lower than whites' by 86.5%. One must keep in mind that when the response variable is log transformed, changing the reference category of a dummy variable leads to two outcomes: The coefficient changes its sign and the percent change is transformed into its reciprocal ($1/e^2 = 1/7.389 = 0.135$ and $0.135 - 1 = -0.865$).

From Log Scale Back to Raw Scale

Log transformation of the response variable provides a technical analytic means by which to obtain a better fit to the data and an interpretation of the

TABLE 6.1
Classical Regression Estimates for
Log Income: Effects of Education and Race

Variable	Coefficient
ED	0.128**
	(0.0020)
WHITE	0.332**
	(0.0160)
Constant	10.497**
	(0.0050)

NOTE: Asymptotic standard errors are in parentheses.

**p < .01

estimates in relative terms. Multiplication on a raw scale becomes addition on a log scale. However, a linear function of a log-transformed response variable specifies the error term as additive rather than multiplicative, thereby altering the distribution of the original error term. In addition, the use of the log transformation has clear disadvantages in that it dramatically distorts the measurement scale. In inequality studies, making a log transformation has the effect of artificially diminishing the appearance of inequality, as it dramatically contracts the right-hand tail of the distribution. Typically, we are more interested in modeling effects on the central location of the raw-scale response variable, rather than on its log transformation.

What do shifts in location of the log-transformed response variable tell us about what happens on the raw-scale response-variable distribution? The answer depends on the choice of location estimate. For the case of the conditional mean, estimates on a log scale provide limited information about what happens on a raw scale, and vice versa. Only *linear* transformations have the equivariance property, enabling the use of the mean of a random variable to determine the mean of its transformation. Because the log transformation is nonlinear, the conditional-mean income is not the exponential function of the conditional mean of log income, as we detailed in Chapter 3. In effect, there is no easy, simple, or closed-form expression to calculate the effect of a covariate in absolute terms from the coefficient of the log-income model. Thus, it is difficult to use the LRM for the log of the response variable to understand the mean shift on the raw scale. In contrast, the median-regression model is more accommodating. When a monotone transformation is applied to the response variable, the conditional median transforms accordingly.

TABLE 6.2

Quantile-Regression Estimates for Log Income: Effects of Education and Race

P	0.05	0.10	0.15	0.20	0.25	0.30	0.35	0.40	0.45	0.50	0.55	0.60	0.65	0.70	0.75	0.80	0.85	0.90	0.95
ED	0.116**	0.131**	0.139**	0.139**	0.140**	0.140**	0.137**	0.136**	0.134**	0.131**	0.128**	0.129**	0.125**	0.124**	0.121**	0.117**	0.116**	0.117**	0.123**
	(0.004)	(0.003)	(0.004)	(0.003)	(0.003)	(0.002)	(0.003)	(0.002)	(0.002)	(0.002)	(0.002)	(0.002)	(0.002)	(0.002)	(0.002)	(0.002)	(0.002)	(0.003)	(0.004)
WHITE	0.429**	0.442**	0.413**	0.399**	0.376**	0.349**	0.346**	0.347**	0.333**	0.323**	0.303**	0.290**	0.295**	0.280**	0.264**	0.239**	0.231**	0.223**	0.222**
	(0.040)	(0.029)	(0.030)	(0.025)	(0.023)	(0.019)	(0.020)	(0.018)	(0.017)	(0.018)	(0.019)	(0.017)	(0.016)	(0.017)	(0.015)	(0.017)	(0.017)	(0.020)	(0.027)
Constant	9.148**	9.494**	9.722**	9.900**	10.048**	10.172**	10.287**	10.391**	10.486**	10.578**	10.671**	10.761**	10.851**	10.939**	11.035**	11.140**	11.255**	11.402**	11.629**
	(0.014)	(0.010)	(0.010)	(0.009)	(0.008)	(0.007)	(0.007)	(0.006)	(0.006)	(0.006)	(0.007)	(0.006)	(0.005)	(0.006)	(0.005)	(0.006)	(0.006)	(0.007)	(0.010)

NOTE: Asymptotic standard errors are in parentheses.

**$p < .01$

More generally, the QRM's monotonic equivariance property guarantees that conditional quantiles of a log-transformed response variable are the log of conditional quantiles of the raw-scale response variable. While the monotonic equivariance property holds at the population level, the retransformation of estimates is more complicated because of the nonlinearity of the log transformation. To complicate matters, for continuous covariates, the rate of change of a quantile of the response variable with respect to a covariate depends on the actual values of the covariate. In the case of a categorical covariate, the effect of changing group membership also depends on the values of the covariates. In either case, it becomes necessary to give a precise meaning to the *effect* of a change in a covariate on quantiles of the response variable. We describe two approaches to addressing this issue. The first of these involves making use of a *typical value* for the covariates, which we call *typical-setting effects* (TSE). The second is *mean effect* (ME), which averages the effect of a covariate on a conditional quantile over all relevant individuals in the population.

Typical-Setting Effect

We are interested in the covariate effect on the response variable in absolute terms, and one way to proceed is to determine this effect for a *typical* setting of the covariates. A relatively straightforward approach is to take this typical setting to be the vector of covariate means. This is a common practice when evaluating effects if the mean of the dependent variable is expressed as a nonlinear function of the covariates.[2]

We illustrate this idea in the two-covariate case. From this, it will be clear how to proceed when the number of covariates is higher. Let x be a continuous covariate (e.g., *ED*) and let d be a dummy covariate (e.g., *WHITE*). For the remainder of this section, we fix a particular p. Under the fitted pth quantile-regression model, we have

$$\hat{Q}^{(p)}(\log y \mid x, d) = \hat{\alpha}^{(p)} + \hat{\beta}_x^{(p)} x + \hat{\beta}_d^{(p)} d, \qquad [6.1]$$

but the constant term $\hat{\alpha}^{(p)}$ can be interpreted as an estimate of the pth quantile of the response when $x = 0$ and $d = 0$. Since the covariates are usually nonnegative, this choice of values is not particularly meaningful, which makes $\hat{\alpha}^{(p)}$ somewhat uninteresting to interpret. On the other hand, if we center all covariates at their means and fit the pth quantile-regression model

$$\hat{Q}^{(p)}(\log y \mid x, d) = \hat{\alpha}^{(p)} + \hat{\beta}_x^{(p)} (x - \bar{x}) + \hat{\beta}_d^{(p)} (d - \bar{d}), \qquad [6.1']$$

this gives rise to a different fitted value for the parameter $\hat{\alpha}^{(p)}$ with a different interpretation: an estimate of the pth quantile of the log-transformed response for the *typical* value of the covariates. The remaining fitted coefficients $\hat{\beta}_x^{(p)}$ and $\hat{\beta}_d^{(p)}$ are the same under Equations 6.1 and 6.1′.

Now consider what happens when we modify one of the covariates, for example, we increase x by one unit from the typical setting while keeping the remaining covariates fixed at their mean levels. The fitted pth quantile of the log response becomes the sum of the constant term and the coefficient of that covariate: $\hat{\alpha} + \hat{\beta}_x$ for x and $\hat{\alpha} + \hat{\beta}_d$ for d.

We wish to know the effect of these modifications on the raw-response scale. The monotonic equivariance property of the QRM tells us that if we know the quantile of a distribution on the log scale, applying the exponential transformation to this quantile gives the quantile on the raw scale. In particular, exponential transformation of the conditional quantile on the log scale for the typical setting leads to a fitted conditional quantile on the raw scale for the typical setting (the mean of all covariates): $e^{\hat{\alpha}}$.[3] Similarly, applying the exponential transformation to log-scale-fitted conditional quantiles under the modified covariate values leads to $e^{\hat{\alpha}+\hat{\beta}_x}$ and $e^{\hat{\alpha}+\hat{\beta}_d}$, respectively. Subtracting the fitted quantile at the typical setting from the conditional quantile modified by a unit change of a covariate yields the raw-scale effect of that covariate, evaluated at the mean of the covariates: $e^{\hat{\alpha}+\hat{\beta}_x} - e^{\hat{\alpha}}$ for x and $e^{\hat{\alpha}+\hat{\beta}_d} - e^{\hat{\alpha}}$ for d. In this manner, we obtain an effect of the covariate on any conditional pth quantile of the response.

In order to understand the potential impact of a covariate on the dependent variable, it is better to retransform log-scale coefficients to raw-scale coefficients. If we were to use the asymptotic procedure, we would have to use the delta method, and the solution would be too complicated without a closed form. It is impractical to use the analytic method to infer these quantities. Instead, we use the flexible bootstrap method (described in Chapter 5) to obtain the standard error and confidence interval of these quantities.

The top panel ("TSE") of Table 6.3 presents in absolute terms the typical-setting effect of *ED* and *WHITE* on income, evaluated at the mean of all covariates, and their 95% confidence interval estimated using bootstrapping. At the median, one more year of schooling above the population mean of education increases income by $5,519, holding race at its mean. Changing group membership from black to white, holding *ED* at its mean, brings about a $15,051 increase in income. The typical-setting effects of both education and race are weaker at the lower tail than at the upper tail. These effects are larger than the results of Table 5.1 when the raw-scale income is fitted. Keep in mind that the income model and log-income model are two different models with different fits. Also, the typical-setting effects are evaluated at the covariate means, whereas the

TABLE 6.3

Point Estimate and 95% Confidence Interval of Typical-Setting Effects and Mean Effects From Log-Income QRM: 500-Resample Bootstrap

| | | ED | | | WHITE | |
| | | CI | | | CI | |
	Effect	Lower Bound	Upper Bound	Effect	Lower Bound	Upper Bound
TSE						
.025	660	530	821	4457	3405	6536
.05	1157	1015	1291	4978	4208	6400
.10	1866	1747	1977	7417	6062	8533
.15	2486	2317	2634	8476	7210	9951
.25	3477	3323	3648	10609	8839	12378
.50	5519	5314	5722	15051	12823	17075
.75	7992	7655	8277	18788	15669	21647
.85	9519	9076	9910	19891	16801	22938
.90	11108	10593	11676	22733	18468	27444
.95	14765	13677	15662	28131	21181	34294
.975	18535	16973	19706	41714	33344	51297
ME						
.025	697	554	887	2719	2243	3424
.05	1241	1073	1396	3276	2875	3868
.10	2028	1887	2163	4792	4148	5284
.15	2717	2514	2903	5613	5007	6282
.25	3799	3620	4008	7228	6343	8098
.50	5965	5716	6203	10746	9528	11832
.75	8524	8114	8865	14141	12162	15828
.85	10082	9581	10559	15429	13362	17329
.90	11772	11157	12478	17664	14900	20491
.95	15754	14476	16810	21875	17207	25839
.975	19836	18007	21235	31419	26192	37014

coefficients from fitting the raw-scale income apply to any covariate settings.

Mean Effect

The *typical-setting* approach is simple to implement and provides some information about the effect of a unit change in a covariate on the response. However, it only accounts for the effect of this change at the mean of the covariates. Since this effect can vary over the range of covariate values, it is plausible that the use of typical values leads to a distorted picture. We introduce another possibility, which is to average in the opposite order: First compute the effect of a unit change in the covariate for every possible setting of the covariates, and then average this effect over the covariate settings in the data. We propose to use this idea when the quantile function of the response depends in a nonlinear way on the covariates, for example, in Equations 6.1 and 6.1′ when log(y) is expressed as a linear function of the covariates. If, instead, the quantile function is a linear function of the covariates, then these two methods of averaging lead to the same result.

Proceeding formally, for a continuous covariate x and for any p, we ask: How much does a (random) individual's pth conditional quantile change if his or her x increases by one unit, with other covariates held constant? We then average this change over individuals in a reference population. Continuing with the two-covariate model, we can determine the quantile difference due to a one-unit increase in x as:

$$\Delta Q_x^{(p)} = \hat{Q}^{(p)}(y|x+1, d) - \hat{Q}^{(p)}(y|x, d). \qquad [6.2]$$

And the average quantile difference becomes the mean effect of a unit change in x on y at p, denoted by $ME_x^{(p)}$:

$$ME_x^{(p)} = \frac{1}{n} \sum_{i=1}^{n} \left[\hat{Q}^{(p)}(y_i \mid x_i + 1, d_i) - \hat{Q}^{(p)}(y_i \mid x_i, d_i) \right]. \qquad [6.3]$$

In our model, where log income is a function of education and race, education is an interval variable. Implementing Equation 6.3 requires:

1. obtaining each individual's estimated pth conditional quantile, using $\hat{Q}^{(p)}(y_i|x_i, d_i) = e^{\hat{\alpha}^{(p)} + \hat{\beta}_x^{(p)} x_i + \hat{\beta}_d^{(p)} d_i}$;

2. obtaining the corresponding pth conditional quantile if his or her education increases by one year using $\hat{Q}^{(p)}(y_i|x_i + 1, d_i) = e^{\hat{\alpha}^{(p)} + \hat{\beta}_x^{(p)} (x_i + 1) + \hat{\beta}_d^{(p)} d_i}$;

3. taking the difference between the two terms; and

4. averaging the difference.

For a dichotomous covariate, we wish to know the change in the conditional quantile if a person changes his or her group membership from $d = 0$ to $d = 1$, while keeping other covariates constant. In this case, only the subgroup of $d = 0$ is relevant because an inclusion of the other group will make other covariates change at the same time. Thus, for dichotomous d, the quantile difference becomes:

$$\Delta Q_{d,0,1}^{(p)} = \hat{Q}^{(p)}(y|x, 1) - \hat{Q}^{(p)}(y|x, 0). \qquad [6.4]$$

And the mean effect of d, denoted by $ME_{d,0,1}^{(p)}$, is:

$$ME_{d,0,1}^{(p)} = \frac{1}{n_0} \sum_{i:d_i=0} \left[\hat{Q}^{(p)}(y_i \mid x_i, 1) - \hat{Q}^{(p)}(y_i \mid x_i, 0) \right], \qquad [6.5]$$

where n_0 denotes the number of sampled individuals with $d_i = 0$.

In our example, *WHITE* is a dummy variable. The calculation will be confined to sampled blacks only (*WHITE* = 0). The steps are:

1. obtaining each black's pth conditional quantile, using
    $\hat{Q}^{(p)}(y_i \mid x_i, d_i = 0) = e^{\hat{\alpha}^{(p)} + \hat{\beta}_x^{(p)} x_i}$;

2. obtaining the corresponding pth conditional quantile if a black becomes
    a white using $\hat{Q}^{(p)}(y_i \mid x_i, d_i = 1) = e^{\hat{\alpha}^{(p)} + \hat{\beta}_x^{(p)} x_i + \hat{\beta}_d^{(p)}}$;

3. taking the difference between the two terms; and

4. averaging the difference.

The bottom panel ("ME") of Table 6.3 presents the mean effect of education and race and their 95% confidence interval. The effects of both *ED* and *WHITE* increase with p. The magnitudes of the education effects are similar to the typical-setting effects. However, the mean effects of *WHITE* change more widely with p than the typical-setting effects.

Infinitesimal Effects

For both the typical-setting and mean-effect methods described above, the covariate of interest is changed by a single unit in order to quantify its effect on the response variable. Since both methods are designed so as to address situations when the quantile function of the response is a nonlinear function of the covariates, the calculated effect is generally not proportional to the size of the unit. For example, the unit of education could be half a year rather than a whole year, and the effect of an increase in half a year of schooling need not be equal to half of the effect of an additional year of schooling. In addition, some covariates may be viewed as truly continuous. For example, in a study of health outcomes, we might use income as a covariate.

An alternative approach is to consider the infinitesimal rate of change in the quantile with respect to a covariate, that is, replace a finite difference by a derivative. For example, assuming we fit a model of Equation 6.1 to give $\hat{Q}^{(p)}(y \mid x, d) = e^{\hat{\alpha}^{(p)} + \hat{\beta}_x^{(p)}(x-\bar{x}) + \hat{\beta}_d^{(p)}(d-\bar{d})}$, we have

$$\frac{d}{dx} \hat{Q}^{(p)}(y \mid x, d) = \hat{\beta}_x^{(p)} e^{\hat{\alpha}^{(p)} + \hat{\beta}_x^{(p)}(x-\bar{x}) + \hat{\beta}_d^{(p)}(d-\bar{d})},$$

so that, substituting $x = \bar{x}$ and $d = \bar{d}$, the analog of the typical-setting effect becomes $\frac{d}{dx}\hat{Q}^{(p)}(y|x, d) = \hat{\beta}_x^{(p)} e^{\hat{\alpha}^{(p)}}$. Similarly, the analog of the mean effect takes the form

$$ ME_x^{(p)} = \frac{1}{n} \sum_{i=1}^{n} \frac{d}{dx} \hat{Q}^{(p)}(y | x_i, d_i) = \frac{1}{n} \sum_{i=1}^{n} \hat{\beta}_x^{(p)} e^{\hat{\alpha} + \hat{\beta}_x^{(p)}(x_i - \bar{x}) + \hat{\beta}_d^{(p)}(d_i - \bar{d})}. $$

Graphical View of Log-Scale Coefficients

The graphs of log-scale coefficients are shown in Figure 6.1, which shows the curve for *ED, WHITE,* and the constant from the log-income QRM. The conditional-quantile function of log income at the typical setting in Figure 6.1c has a somewhat normal appearance, given its similar slopes below and above the median. This finding shows that the log transformation of income contracts the right tail so that the posttransformed distribution is closer to normal. Since a log coefficient can be interpreted as a percentage change, a straight horizontal line should indicate a pure scale shift without a skewness shift. Any curves departing from the horizontal pattern can indicate either skewness shifts or pure location shifts, but it is very difficult to tell which

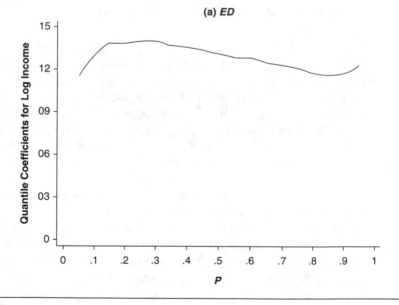

Figure 6.1   Graphical View of Log-Scale Estimates From Log-Income QRM

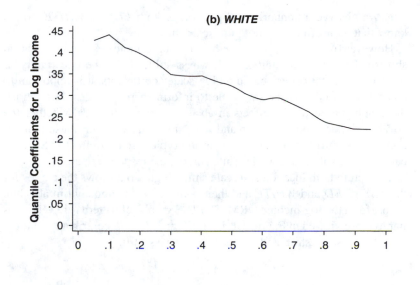

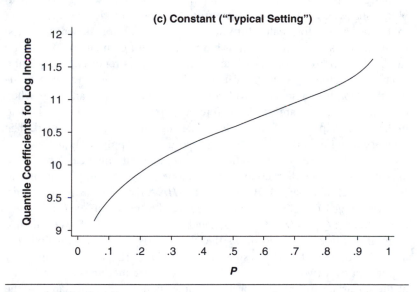

Figure 6.1 (Continued)

one. We observe a nonhorizontal pattern for both *ED* and *WHITE,* so we know that their effects are not pure scale shifts.

However, we are not sure whether the curve indicates a pure location shift or if there is an additional skewness shift. Given the uncertainty of the nonhorizontal pattern based on log-scale coefficients, it is important to reconstruct effects on the raw scale to inform shape changes. In contrast, the graphs based on the effects in absolute terms can reveal whether the covariate induces both location and scale shifts and whether it also induces a skewness shift. For example, using the typical-setting effect (TSE), we can view the role of a covariate in changing the response shape.

To capture both location and scale shifts, Figure 6.2 shows the curves for the TSE of *ED* and *WHITE* and their confidence envelope, all in absolute terms, from the log-income QRM. The TSE graphical patterns are very similar to those viewed in Figure 5.1. Both *ED* and *WHITE* contribute to a location shift, a scale shift, and a possible skewness shift.

Shape-Shift Measures From Log-Scale Fits

Because shape shifts are easier to interpret on the raw scale, it is best to obtain shape shifts on the raw scale from log-scale coefficients. According to Equation 5.1 for scale shifts and Equation 5.2 for skewness shifts, the reference's scale and skewness are necessary for comparison. When the raw-scale response variable is fitted, the coefficients represent a departure from any reference. However, when the log-scale response variable is fitted, the departure associated with a change in a covariate can differ when different references are used. Therefore, a fixed reference is required to understand shape shifts when a log-scale response variable is fitted. The typical-setting effects can serve this purpose well. Applying Equations 5.1 and 5.2 to the TSE results in Table 6.3, we compute the scale shifts and skewness shifts and their confidence envelope using bootstrap resamples in the top panel of Table 6.4. Both *ED* and *WHITE* have a positive scale shift over the range of $Q_{.025}$ to $Q_{.975}$ and a negative skewness shift over the ranges of $Q_{.25}$ to $Q_{.75}$, $Q_{.10}$ to $Q_{.90}$, $Q_{.05}$ to $Q_{.95}$, and $Q_{.025}$ to $Q_{.975}$. The 95% confidence interval of these measures shows that the *SKC* is significant for both *ED* and *WHITE,* while the *SKS* is significant for all four ranges for *ED* and only significant over two ranges for *WHITE*. Since these measures are evaluated at the covariate means and the log-income model is not the same as the income model, the measures' magnitudes should differ from those measures found in Chapter 5. Nonetheless, we should expect that the sign of the shifts and the overall pattern should remain the same. Whether income or

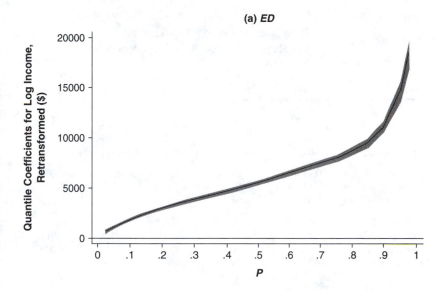

(a) *ED*

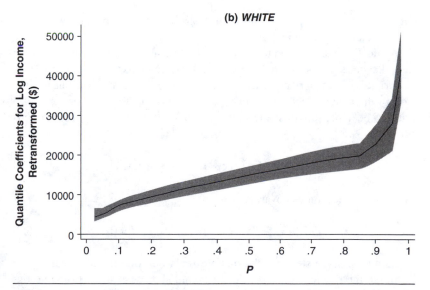

(b) *WHITE*

Figure 6.2 Graphical View of TSE (in Absolute Terms) From Log-Income QRM

TABLE 6.4

Point Estimate and 95% Confidence

Interval of Shape Shifts: 500-Resample Bootstrap

Variable	SCS (.025 to .975)	SKS (.025 to .975)	SKS (.05 to .95)	SKS (.10 to .90)	SKS (.25 to .75)
TSE-Based					
ED	17861	−.016	−.017	−.025	−.015
Lower Bound	16325	−.028	−.029	−.036	−.029
Upper Bound	19108	−.006	−.006	−.014	−.002
WHITE	37113	−.040	−.118	−.111	−.090
Lower Bound	29014	−.129	−.194	−.193	−.199
Upper Bound	46837	.054	−.022	−.015	.047
ME-Based					
ED	19118	−.016	−.017	−.025	−.015
Lower Bound	17272	−.028	−.030	−.036	−.029
Upper Bound	20592	−.006	−.006	−.014	−.002
WHITE	28653	−.046	−.114	−.107	−.084
Lower Bound	23501	−.128	−.181	−.175	−.174
Upper Bound	34348	.042	−.030	−.026	.031

log income is fitted, the location and shape shifts associated with each covariate are not in sync.

While TSE can be used to directly calculate a covariate's effect on scale and skewness shifts, mean effects cannot. Nonetheless, the derivation of a covariate's effect on scale shifts and skewness shifts is similar to the derivation of the mean effect itself. Let S be a shape measure (scale or skewness) and ΔS be a measure of shape shifts. The derivation of ΔS for a continuous covariate is:

$$\Delta S_x^{(p)} = S^{(p)}(y \mid x+1, \, d) - S^{(p)}(y \mid x, d),$$ [6.6]

and for a dichotomous covariate it is:

$$\Delta S_{d,0,1}^{(p)} = S^{(p)}(y, \, d=1) - S^{(p)}(y \mid x, \, d=0).$$ [6.7]

Using the same steps for the mean effects on conditional quantiles, we compute the mean effect on scale shifts and skewness shifts from the log-income QRM (see the bottom panel of Table 6.4). One more year of schooling contributes to a positive scale shift, which is similar to that based on the

TSE. *WHITE* has a positive effect on scale shifts, and the magnitude is larger than that based on the TSE. The effects of education and race on skewness shifts are remarkably similar between ME and TSE. The overall pattern given by the ME is also not in sync, supporting the same conclusion as when using the TSE.

Summary

This chapter discusses interpretation issues arising from nonlinear, monotone transformation of the response variable in the QRM. Thanks to the monotone equivariance of the QRM, we are able to reconstruct the effects of a covariate on the raw scale of the response distribution, which is unachievable with the LRM. Nonetheless, the reconstruction requires specific methods. This chapter develops two approaches. The typical-setting method is computationally simple, while the mean-effect method is slightly more involved. Both approaches involve averaging over the covariate values, but in different orders. Both typical-setting effects and mean effects refer to the whole sample or a subsample. Researchers should choose a method that best addresses a specific research question.

The next chapter provides an overall summary of the techniques introduced in this book by applying them to a real research question. In the application, we compare the sources of U.S. income inequality in 1991 and 2001, illustrating what motivates a QR analysis and how to proceed step by step, with the complete Stata codes.

Notes

1. If the estimate coefficient is $\hat{\beta}$, then a unit increase in the predictor variable results in an increase of $(100(e^{\beta} - 1))\%$. For *small* values of the estimated coefficient $\hat{\beta}$, this is approximately $100\hat{\beta}\%$.

2. These practices include the effect on probability from logit-, probit-, and tobit-model estimates.

3. For linear-regression models, the fitted intercept can be interpreted as the geometric mean of the response y. The geometric mean is defined as $\left(\prod_{i}^{n} y_i\right)^{\frac{1}{n}}$, which is equivalent to $e^{\frac{1}{n}\left(\sum_{i}^{n} \log y_i\right)}$. The geometric mean is always less than or equal to the arithmetic mean. But this interpretation is no longer valid in quantile regression.

7. APPLICATION TO INCOME
INEQUALITY IN 1991 AND 2001

The empirical illustrations in previous chapters used oversimplified specifications with one or two covariates. This chapter applies the techniques in the book to a particular topic: the persistence and widening of household income inequality from 1991 to 2001. Our goal is to systematically summarize the techniques developed in this book via a concrete empirical application. Drawing from the U.S. Survey of Income and Program Participation (SIPP), we add the 1991 data to the previously used 2001 data. Household income is adjusted to the 2001 constant dollar. We specify a parsimonious model for household income as a function of five factors (13 covariates): life cycle (age and age-squared), race-ethnicity (white, black, Hispanic, and Asian), education (college graduate, some college, high school graduate, and without high-school education), household types (married couple with children, married couple without children, female head with children, single person, and other), and rural residence. This is the specification used throughout the chapter. Models for both raw-scale income and log-transformed income are fitted. The analyses include (a) assessing the goodness of fit for raw-scale and log-scale income models, (b) comparing ordinary-least-squares (OLS) and median-regression estimates, (c) examining coefficients at the two tails, (d) graphically viewing 19 sets of coefficient estimates and their confidence intervals, and (e) attaining location and shape shifts of conditional quantiles for each covariate in each year and examining the trend over the decade.

Observed Income Disparity

Figure 7.1 shows 99 empirical quantiles for race-ethnicity groups and education groups in 1991 and 2001. One of the most interesting features is the greater spread for the middle 98% of the members in each group in 2001 as compared to 1991.

More detailed comparisons require the actual values of the quantiles. Table 7.1 compares the .025th-quantile, median, and .975th-quantile household incomes (in 2001 constant dollars) for 1991 and 2001. The numbers are weighted to reflect population patterns. A common characteristic is observed for the total and each subgroup: The stretch ($QSC_{.025}$) for the middle 95% households is much wider for 2001 than for 1991, indicating growing total and within-group disparities in income over the decade.

The racial disparity between whites and others in the lower half of the income distribution declined in the last decade. This decline can be seen as

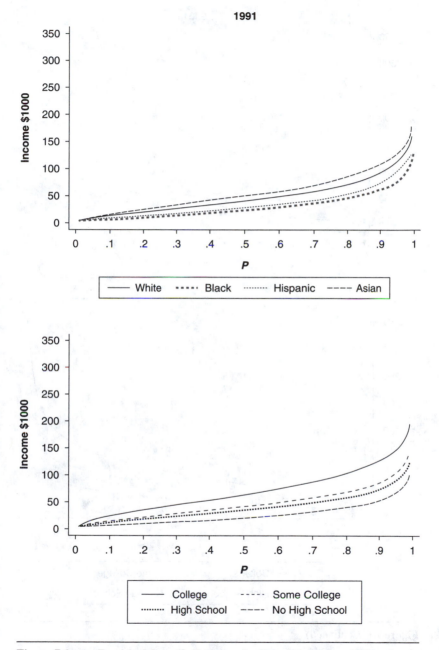

Figure 7.1   Empirical Quantile Functions by Race-Ethnicity and Education Groups

(Continued)

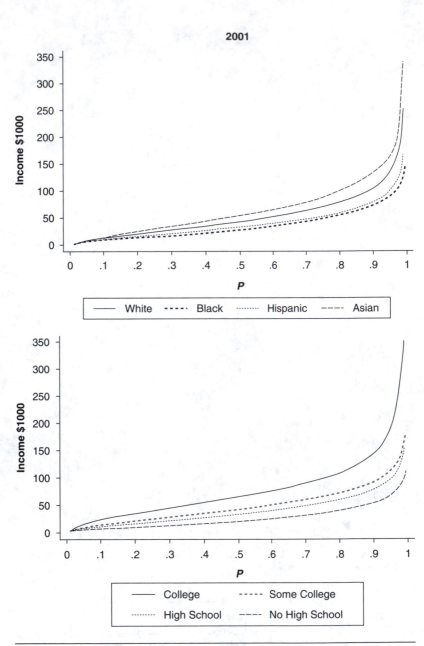

2001

Figure 7.1 (Continued)

TABLE 7.1

Household Income Distribution by Groups: 1991 and 2001

Group	Quantile					
	1991			2001		
	.025	.500	.975	.025	.500	.975
Total	6256	38324	131352	6000	40212	164323
Race-Ethnicity						
White	6765	40949	135443	6600	42878	172784
Black	3773	23624	101160	3788	27858	113124
Hispanic	5342	28851	114138	5600	33144	119454
Asian	5241	49354	149357	4800	55286	211112
Education						
College graduate	11196	64688	168912	10910	65298	263796
Some college	8059	42082	120316	6364	41901	134796
High school grad.	6392	35723	104102	5347	33246	118162
No high school	4918	20827	80603	4408	20319	79515
Household Type						
Married w/ children	12896	55653	143343	14193	61636	204608
Married w/o children	11621	43473	146580	10860	47665	176375
Female head	3666	23420	94114	3653	27690	96650
Single person	4884	20906	83213	3977	21369	91551
Other household type	7301	37896	115069	6600	41580	150123
Residence						
Urban	6330	40732	137574	6199	42504	174733
Rural	6122	32874	111891	5419	33505	118079

the fall in the .025th-quantile income of white households in contrast with a moderate gain for the black and Hispanic counterparts. Asians made greater headway than whites at the median and at the .975th quantile, but the lowest 2.5% of Asian households were left behind.

An important change in income inequality is the change in returns to education for the top tail. While most college graduates gained an ample amount of income over the decade, more than half of the people with a below-college education saw their income actually decline. In particular, more than 97.5% of high school dropouts in 2001 had a notably lower income than their 1991 counterparts.

Consideration of household type, defined by marriage and presence of children, leads us to another arena where social stratification reshapes the income distribution. Progress is seen for married couples with children, whereas the income of single-mother families and single-person households is stagnant. Inequality between urban and rural areas and inequality within both urban and rural areas intensified over the decade studied.

Descriptive Statistics

Table 7.2 presents the weighted mean and standard deviation for variables used in the analyses. We see that mean income increased by nearly $5,000 from 1991 to 2001, a much higher figure than the growth in median income observed in the previous table. The small increase in log income reminds us that the log transformation contracts the right tail of the distribution. We observe greater diversity in the race-ethnicity structure and considerable improvement in the population's education. However, the number of households of married couples with children decreased, whereas "other" types and single-person households were on the rise. The United States continued the urbanization and suburbanization seen in previous decades.

TABLE 7.2
Descriptive Statistics of Variables Used in Analysis

	1991		2001	
Variable	Mean	SD	Mean	SD
Response				
Income ($)	46168	33858	51460	46111
Log income	10.451	0.843	10.506	0.909
Age	49	17	49	17
Age-squared	2652	1798	2700	1786
Covariate				
Race-Ethnicity				
White	.795	.404	.755	.430
Black	.101	.301	.118	.322
Hispanic	.079	.269	.094	.292
Asian	.025	.157	.033	.177
Education				
College graduate	.230	.421	.261	.439
Some college	.210	.407	.296	.457
High school grad.	.341	.474	.302	.459
No high school	.219	.414	.141	.348
Household Type				
Married w/ children	.330	.470	.287	.452
Married w/o children	.224	.417	.233	.423
Female head	.108	.310	.104	.305
Single person	.257	.437	.267	.442
Other household type	.082	.274	.110	.313
Residence				
Urban	.732	.443	.773	.419
Rural	.268	.443	.227	.419
Sample Size	10111		25891	

Notes on Survey Income Data

Two characteristics of survey income data make the QRM approach a better strategy for analysis than the LRM. First, only 0.2% of the households have incomes over a million dollars, whereas for over 96% of the population, income is less than $100,000. Thus, data for the very rich profoundly influence the OLS coefficient estimates. Second, survey income is often top-coded for each income source; thus, it is not straightforward to assess at which level a household's *total* income is trimmed. In addition, surveys in different years may use different top-coding criteria, resulting in a tedious process to make the data from different years comparable. These problems are not concerns in quantile-regression modeling owing to the robustness property of the QRM described in Chapter 3. In this example, we choose the two extremes to be the .025th and .975th quantiles, thus focusing on modeling the middle 95% of the population. Since data points that have been top-coded tend to be associated with *positive* residuals for the fitted .975th QRM, the effect on the QRM estimates of replacing the (unknown) income values with top-coded values tends to be minimal. This simplifies data management since we can include in the analysis all survey data points, top-coded or not.

Throughout this example, each covariate is centered at its mean. Consequently, the constant term from the income OLS regression represents the mean income of the population, whereas the constant term from the log-income OLS regression represents the mean log income. For the fitted QRM models based on centered covariates, the constant term for the income quantile regression represents the conditional quantile for income at the typical setting, and the constant term for the log income represents the conditional quantile for log income at the typical setting.

Goodness of Fit

Because the QRM no longer makes linear-regression assumptions, raw-scale income can be used without transformation. Nevertheless, we would like to choose a better-fitting model if log transformation can achieve it. We thus perform comparisons of goodness of fit between the income equation and the log-income equation. We fit separate QRMs at the 19 equally spaced quantiles (a total of $2 \times 19 = 38$ fits), using Stata's "qreg" command. Although the qreg command produces the asymptotic standard errors (which can be biased), we are only interested in the goodness-of-fit statistics, the QRM Rs. Table 7.3 shows the QRM's Rs (defined in Chapter 5) for the raw- and log-scale response.

In general, log transformation yields a better fit of the model to the data than the raw scale. For the 1991 data, the R of log income is higher for

$0 < p < .65$—nearly two thirds of the 19 quantiles examined gain a better fit. For the 2001 data, the R of log income is higher for $0 < p < .85$, presenting a stronger case for using log transformation for the 2001 data than for the 1991 data. However, the log scale does not fit as well at the top tail. If the top-tail behavior and stratification are the major concern, the raw-scale income should be used. For this reason, we will illustrate analyses of both scales.

Conditional-Mean Versus Conditional-Median Regression

We model the conditional median to represent the relationship between the central location of income and the covariates. By contrast, conditional-mean models, such as the OLS, estimate the conditional mean, which tends to capture the upper tail of the (right-skewed) income distribution. The median regression was estimated using the Stata "qreg" command. This command was also used on 500 bootstrap samples of the original sample so

TABLE 7.3
Goodness of Fit: Raw-Scale Versus Log-Scale Income QRM

	1991			2001		
	Income	Log Income	Difference	Income	Log Income	Difference
Quantile	(1)	(2)	(2) − (1)	(1)	(2)	(2) − (1)
.05	.110	.218	.109	.093	.194	.101
.10	.155	.264	.109	.130	.237	.107
.15	.181	.281	.099	.154	.255	.101
.20	.198	.286	.088	.173	.265	.091
.25	.212	.290	.078	.188	.270	.083
.30	.224	.290	.067	.200	.274	.074
.35	.233	.290	.057	.209	.276	.066
.40	.242	.289	.048	.218	.277	.059
.45	.249	.288	.039	.225	.276	.051
.50	.256	.286	.029	.231	.275	.044
.55	.264	.282	.019	.236	.273	.037
.60	.270	.279	.009	.240	.270	.030
.65	.275	.275	−.001	.243	.266	.023
.70	.280	.270	−.010	.246	.262	.015
.75	.285	.264	−.021	.249	.256	.008
.80	.291	.258	−.032	.249	.250	.000
.85	.296	.250	−.047	.250	.242	−.008
.90	.298	.237	−.061	.252	.233	−.019
.95	.293	.213	−.080	.258	.222	−.036

NOTE: Presented are R-squared of QRM.

as to obtain the bootstrap standard error (see Appendix for Stata codes for this computing task). Table 7.4 lists the OLS estimates and median-regression estimates for raw-scale and log-scale income in 2001. We expect that the effects based on OLS would appear stronger than effects based on median regression because of the influence of the data in the upper-income tail on OLS coefficients.

While the coefficients of the income equation are in absolute terms, the log-income coefficients are in relative terms. With a few exceptions, the

TABLE 7.4
OLS and Median Regression: 2001 Raw and Log Income

	OLS		Median	
Variable	Coeff.	SE	Coeff.	BSE
Income				
Age	2191	(84.1)	1491	(51.4)
Age-squared	−22	(.8)	−15	(.5)
Black	−9800	(742.9)	−7515	(420.7)
Hispanic	−9221	(859.3)	−7620	(551.3)
Asian	−764	(1369.3)	−3080	(1347.9)
Some college	−24996	(643.7)	−18551	(612.5)
High school grad.	−32281	(647.4)	−24939	(585.6)
No high school	−38817	(830.0)	−30355	(616.4)
Married w/o children	−11227	(698.5)	−11505	(559.6)
Female head	−28697	(851.1)	−25887	(580.2)
Single person	−37780	(684.3)	−32012	(504.8)
Other household type	−14256	(837.3)	−13588	(672.8)
Rural residence	−10391	(560.7)	−6693	(344.1)
Constant	50431	(235.2)	43627	(185.5)
Log Income				
Age	0.0500	(.0016)	0.0515	(.0016)
Age-squared	−0.0005	(.00002)	−0.0005	(.00001)
Black	−0.2740	(.0140)	−0.2497	(.0145)
Hispanic	−0.1665	(.0162)	−0.1840	(.0185)
Asian	−0.1371	(.0258)	−0.0841	(.0340)
Some college	−0.3744	(.0121)	−0.3407	(.0122)
High school grad.	−0.5593	(.0122)	−0.5244	(.0123)
No high school	−0.8283	(.0156)	−0.8011	(.0177)
Married w/o children	−0.1859	(.0132)	−0.1452	(.0124)
Female head	−0.6579	(.0160)	−0.6214	(.0167)
Single person	−0.9392	(.0129)	−0.8462	(.0136)
Other household type	−0.2631	(.0158)	−0.2307	(.0166)
Rural residence	−0.1980	(.0106)	−0.1944	(.0100)
Constant	10.4807	(.0044)	10.5441	(.0045)

NOTE: BSE is bootstrap standard error based on 500 replicates.

OLS coefficients for log income are larger in magnitude than for median regression. For example, compared with being white, being black decreases the conditional-median income by $100(e^{-.274}-1) = -24\%$ according to the OLS results, but by $100(e^{-.2497} - 1) = -22\%$ according to the median-regression results. In other words, mean income for blacks is 24% lower than it is for whites, and blacks' median income is 22% lower than whites', all else being equal. We note that while we can determine the effect of being black in absolute terms on the conditional median because of the monotonic equi-variance property of the QRM, we cannot do so with the conditional-mean log-scale estimates because the LRM does not have the monotonic equi-variance property. We will later return to attaining effects in absolute terms from log-income-equation estimates.

Graphical View of QRM Estimates From Income and Log-Income Equations

An important departure of the QRM from the LRM is that there are numerous sets of quantile coefficients being estimated. We use Stata's "sqreg" command for fitting the QRM with 19 equally spaced quantiles (.05th, . . . , .95th) simultaneously. The sqreg command uses the bootstrap method to estimate the standard errors of these coefficients. We specified 500 replicates to ensure a large enough number of bootstrap samples for stable estimates of the standard errors and 95% confidence intervals. The sqreg command does not save estimates from each bootstrap but only presents a summary of the results. We perform this bootstrapping for raw-scale income and log-transformed income. Results from the sqreg are used to make graphical presentations of coefficients.

Using such a large number of estimates results in a trade-off between complexity and parsimony. On the one hand, the large numbers of parameter estimates are capable of capturing complex and subtle changes in the distribution shape, which is exactly the advantage of using the QRM. On the other hand, this complexity is not without costs, as we may be confronted with an unwieldy collection of coefficient estimates to interpret. Thus, a graphical view of QRM estimates, previously optional, becomes a necessary step in interpreting QRM results.

We are particularly interested in how the effect of a covariate varies with the quantiles of interest. The graphical view in which we plot how the estimated QRM coefficients vary with p is valuable for highlighting trends in these coefficients. For raw-scale coefficients, a horizontal line indicates that the coefficient does not vary with p, so that the effect of a constant change in the covariate on the quantile of the response is the same for all quantiles.

In other words, with all the other covariates fixed, the covariate change produces a pure location shift: a positive shift if the line is above the horizontal zero line and a negative shift if the line is below the zero line. On the other hand, a straight nonhorizontal line indicates both location and scale shifts. In this case, the location shift is determined by the quantile coefficient at the median: A positive median coefficient indicates a rightward location shift and a negative median coefficient indicates a leftward location shift. An upward-sloping straight line indicates a positive scale shift (the scale becomes wider). By contrast, a downward-sloping straight line indicates a negative scale shift (the scale becomes narrower). Any nonlinear appearance in the curve implies the presence of a more complex shape shift, for example, in the form of a skewness shift. These graphs, however, provide neither exact quantities of shape shifts nor their statistical significance. We will examine their significance later using shape-shift quantities.

To illustrate how to identify the location and shape shifts using a graphical view, we examine closely the age effect on raw-scale income in Figure 7.2. As the coefficients and the confidence envelope are above 0 (the thick horizontal line), the age effects on various quantiles of raw-scale income are all positive and significant. The age coefficients form an upward-sloping, generally straight line, indicating that an increase in age shifts the location of the income distribution rightward and expands the scale of the income distribution.

The plots in Figure 7.3 show results for raw-scale income. Coefficient point estimates and 95% confidence intervals based on bootstrap standard errors are plotted against $p \in (0,1)$. The shaded area indicates that the effect of a covariate is significant for particular quantiles if the area does not cross zero. For example, the Asian effect is insignificant beyond $p > .45$ because the confidence envelope crosses 0 beyond that point. Chapter 4 summarizes some basic patterns that provide hints as to location shifts and scale shifts for raw- and log-scale coefficients. Below we discuss patterns emerging from our example.

The graph for the constant coefficient is a predicted quantile function for income for the *typical* household (i.e., the income of a fictional household based on the mean of all covariates) and serves as the baseline. This quantile function indicates that for the typical household, income has a right-skewed distribution. This skewness is less pronounced than the skewness observed for the income data without taking into account the effects of the covariates. Among the 13 covariates, only "age" has positive effects. The middle 70% of the population is estimated to have a proportional increase in income with age. The bottom-tail rates of the age effect are disproportionately lower, whereas the upper-tail rates are disproportionately higher. However, this nonproportionality is not sufficient to allow conclusions about skewness, because

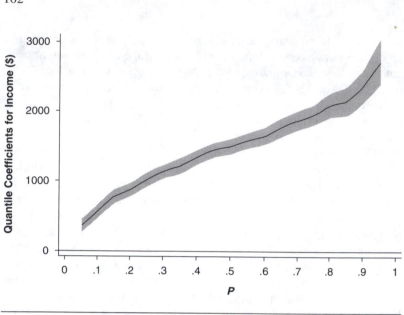

Figure 7.2   Age Effect: Raw-Scale QRM Coefficient and Bootstrap
Confidence Envelope, 2001

the baseline skewness (represented by the constant term) must be taken into
account. All other covariates have negative effects. As mentioned earlier, the
Asian effect is significant for the lower tail of the conditional distribution.
This segment of the curves is quite flat, suggesting a pure location shift
for the lower half. A few covariates have close-to-flat curves; for example,
compared with whites, Hispanics' income is lower by a similar amount at
almost all quantiles, making the curve flat. However, most covariates appear
to produce not only location shifts but also substantial shape shifts.

The graphs for log coefficients are presented in Figure 7.4. We note that
log transformation contracts the right-skewed distribution to give approximate normality. Thus, the graph of the constant coefficients resembles the
quantile function of a normal distribution. As discussed in Chapter 4,
the log coefficient approximates proportional change in relative terms;
straight flat lines indicate location shifts and scale shifts without changing
the skewness. Any departure from the straight flat line becomes difficult to
interpret as it tends to indicate combinations of location, scale, and skewness shifts. In addition, because on the log scale a tiny amount of log
income above or below a straight flat line at the upper quantiles translates
to a large amount of income, we should be cautious in claiming a close-to-
flat curve. For example, the curves for the three lowest categories of education appear quite flat, but we do not claim them as close-to-flat because

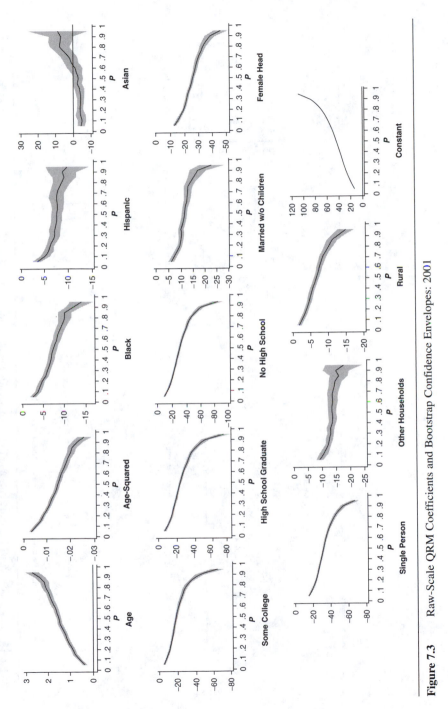

Figure 7.3 Raw-Scale QRM Coefficients and Bootstrap Confidence Envelopes: 2001

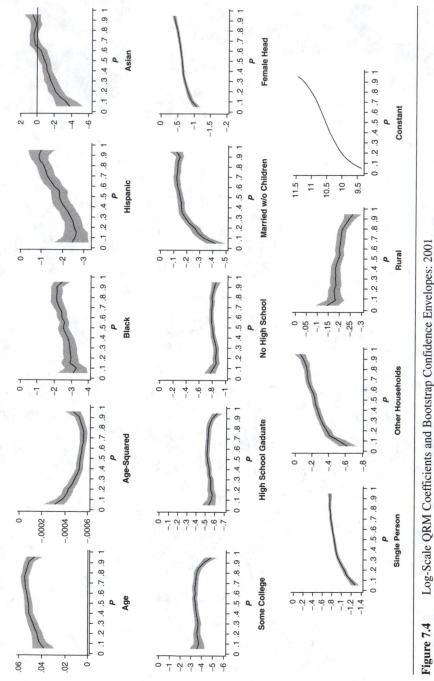

Figure 7.4 Log-Scale QRM Coefficients and Bootstrap Confidence Envelopes: 2001

their upper tail above the .8th quantile drops discernibly. In short, graphs of log coefficients are less telling and require greater caution in interpretation than graphs of raw-scale coefficients.

Quantile Regressions at Noncentral Positions: Effects in Absolute Terms

Graphical views offer an overview of the covariates' impact on the shape of the conditional-income distribution. We now complement the graphical view with a closer look at some of the off-central positions. We choose two extremes that fall outside of the graphs we just examined: the .025th and .975th quantiles. In order to obtain coefficient standard errors for these additional .025th- and .975th-quantile regressions of raw-scale income, we can either use "sqreg" with 500 replicates or manually perform the boot-strap method for 500 replicates, saving all 500 sets of resulting coefficient estimates. The conditional shape-shift quantities require programming based on each of the bootstrap replicates of these two quantile estimates, so we present the manual bootstrap results here. With the 500 sets of coeffi-cient estimates, we use the median as the point estimate and the middle 95% as the confidence interval. If the confidence interval does not cross 0, the coefficient is significant at the $p = .05$ level. These results are almost identical to the sqreq outputs.

Estimates for the log-income equations are not in absolute terms. Because effects in absolute terms are essential to understanding the impact of a covariate on the shape of the distribution, we need to find the effect in absolute terms, evaluated at the typical setting (the mean of all covariates). As for the raw income, we save 500 sets of log-scale coefficients from boot-strap samples. For each covariate in the estimation based on a bootstrap sample, we

- Obtain the log-conditional quantile of one unit increase from the mean of the covariate by adding the coefficient to the constant term.
- Take the exponential of this log-conditional quantile and the exponential of the constant term to yield two raw-scale conditional quantiles.
- Take the difference between these two raw-scale-conditional quantiles, which becomes the effect of the covariate in absolute terms, evaluated at the typical setting, the TSE.

Table 7.5 shows the effects in absolute terms from income and log-income equations at the .025th and .975th quantiles. The top panel is from the income equation. The constant term represents the estimated value of

TABLE 7.5
Effects in Absolute Terms on Tail Quantiles:
2001 Raw and Log Income

	0.025th Quantile	0.975th Quantile
Variable	Coeff.	Coeff.
Income Model		
Age	248**	3103**
Age-squared	−2**	−29**
Black	−1991**	−17380**
Hispanic	−2495**	−7418
Asian	−4221**	16235
Some college	−2607**	−105858**
High school grad.	−4332**	−119924**
No high school	−6211**	−129464**
Married w/o children	−4761**	−18878**
Female head	−10193**	−50465**
Single person	−12257**	−78570**
Other household type	−7734**	−16876**
Rural residence	−943**	−18654**
Constant	10156**	137561**
Log-Income Model		
Age	396**	5409**
Age-squared	−3**	−53**
Black	−2341**	−28867**
Hispanic	−1835**	−8032
Asian	−3259**	8636
Some college	−1916**	−49898**
High school grad.	−2932**	−57557**
No high school	−4095**	−70006**
Married w/o children	−3149**	−12471**
Female head	−5875**	−33219**
Single person	−6409**	−63176**
Other household type	−4382**	−5282**
Rural residence	−938**	−26742**
Constant	8457**	115804**

NOTE: Significance (** $p < .05$) is determined by 95% confidence interval based on 500 bootstrap replicates.

the .025th and .975th quantiles, respectively, when all covariates are at their mean values: about $10,000 at the bottom and about $137,000 at the top. The most striking pattern is the huge difference in the effect of a covariate on the two ends. For example, being black reduces income by $1,991 at the .025th quantile and by $17,380 at the .975th quantile. In addition, Hispanics and Asians have significantly lower income than whites at the .025th quantile but not at the .975th percentile.

The lower panel shows the TSEs based on the log-income equation. The constant term represents the .025th and .975th conditional quantiles at the typical setting. The TSEs are quite similar to those estimated from the income equation. They are not exactly the same, because the log-income model fits better than the income model and because the log-income equation estimates are evaluated at the typical setting.

Assessing a Covariate's Effect
on Location and Shape Shifts

QRM estimates can be used to calculate precisely how a covariate shifts the location and shape of the conditional distribution. To do such an assessment, we compare two groups: a reference group and a comparison group. In the case of a continuous covariate, the reference group is defined by equating the covariate to some value, and the comparison group is defined by increasing the covariate by one unit, holding other covariates constant. For a dichotomous covariate, we change its value from 0 to 1, holding other covariates constant. All comparisons are made in absolute terms to reveal the raw-scale distribution. Thus, if log-income regression is used to fit the data, the coefficient in absolute terms for a covariate is obtained first (as in the previous section). Location shifts are captured by the coefficients at the median. Shape (scale and skewness) shifts are based on a combination of a number of coefficients. Their significance levels are determined using the bootstrap method.

Table 7.6 shows the results from the income model for 1991 and 2001, with location shifts in the top panel, scale shifts in the middle, and skewness shifts in the bottom. In 1991, all covariates except Asian significantly shift the comparison group's location from the reference group. Some of these effects change noticeably from 1991 to 2001. The Asian location shift, insignificant in 1991, becomes significantly negative in 2001, suggesting the absolute advantage of whites over minorities. Other racial and ethnic groups' location shifts, however, appear to become weaker. Age's location shift is less important in 2001 than in 1991. The same is true for having less education. However, the negative location shifts for household types that are not "married with children" become stronger, as does rural residence.

Location shifts capture between-group differences. As previously discussed for Table 7.4, median-regression coefficients are weaker than OLS coefficients. For the highly right-skewed income distribution, median-regression coefficients capture the central location shift, whereas the OLS coefficients are influenced more heavily by the right tail. Using location shifts (median regression), our findings regarding education groups suggest that the

TABLE 7.6
Location and Shape Shifts of Conditional
Quantiles: From Raw-Scale QRM

Shift	1991	2001
Location Shift		
Age	1801**	1501**
Age-squared	−169**	−149**
Black	−7878**	−7473**
Hispanic	−8692**	−7616**
Asian	−1231	−2850**
Some college	−19173**	−18588**
High school grad.	−25452**	−24926**
No high school	−32595**	−30345**
Married w/o children	−9562**	−11501**
Female head	−22366**	−25862**
Single person	−27866**	−32039**
Other household type	−11716**	−13659**
Rural residence	−5284**	−6698**
Scale Shift (middle 95% of population)		
Age	3393**	2852**
Age-squared	−305**	−272**
Black	−14617**	−15378**
Hispanic	−3027	−4893
Asian	11425	20842
Some college	−34212**	−103245**
High school grad.	−49002**	−115600**
No high school	−63477**	−123369**
Married w/o children	3708	−14001**
Female head	−9177	−40290**
Single person	−32482**	−66374**
Other household type	−8220	−8819**
Rural residence	−9817**	−17693**
Skewness Shift (middle 95% of population)		
Age	−0.0200**	−0.0195**
Age-squared	0.0003**	0.0002**
Black	0.0242	0.0713
Hispanic	0.2374**	0.1833**
Asian	0.0395	0.1571
Some college	0.3524**	−0.8572
High school grad.	0.5245**	−1.0263
No high school	0.7447**	−1.1890
Married w/o children	0.4344**	0.1514
Female head	0.8493**	0.3781**
Single person	0.5229**	0.2184
Other household type	0.1748	0.1714
Rural residence	0.0446	0.0541

NOTE: Significance (** $p < .05$) is determined by 95% confidence interval based on 500 bootstrap replicates.

education effect in terms of location shifts is not as strong as indicated in the literature. The change in location shift, or between-group difference, is only one part of the story about how inequality changed over the decade; the other is the shape change, or relative within-group differences. The advantage of the QRM is that they disentangle the between- and within-group differences, advancing our understanding of changes in inequality.

Scale shifts are one type of shape changes. Among the three racial and ethnic minority groups, only blacks have a shorter conditional-income distribution scale than do whites. The scale for the income of the middle 95% of blacks is much narrower than it is for whites, suggesting greater homogeneity among blacks than whites and the significance of race in determining income. This scale shift becomes stronger in 2001. The same is seen in the three less-educated groups. The education scale shift offers a consistent and refined finding about the increasing importance of education in determining income: It is the shape shift, rather than the location shift, that indicates the rising importance of education.

Skewness shifts are another type of shape change. An increase in the skewness of a conditional quantile indicates uneven within-group differentiation that favors the top-tail members. The 1991 results show that many disadvantaged groups experience this uneven within-group differentiation, including Hispanics, the three less-educated groups, and disadvantaged household types (single-mother, single-person, and "other" households). Some of these shifts disappear in 2001, particularly those of the education groups. This finding further reveals the mechanism by which society rewards college graduates and limits upward mobility for the most able among the less educated.

Results on the raw scale from the log-income model are shown in Table 7.7. These results capture the same trends for life cycle, racial and ethnic groups, education groups, household types, and rural residence. The location shifts and scale shifts in each year, as well as their decade trends, are similar whether income or log income is fitted. Discrepancies are found for skewness shifts. In particular, skewness is reduced significantly for less-educated groups in 2001; this finding is significant based on the log-income model but insignificant based on the income model. It is not surprising that such discrepancies should appear when examining the two model fits (income and log income). They represent fundamentally distinct models, with one of them (log income) providing a better fit. On the other hand, if qualitative conclusions differ, it may indicate that the results are sensitive. We determine whether this is the case by looking at the overall evaluation of a covariate's role in inequality.

We develop an overall evaluation of a covariate's impact on inequality, which examines the alignment of the signs of location and shape shifts.

TABLE 7.7

Location and Shape Shifts of
Conditional Quantiles: From Log-Scale QRM

Shift	1991	2001
Location Shift		
Age	2456**	1994**
Age-squared	−24**	−20**
Black	−9759**	−8386**
Hispanic	−7645**	−6300**
Asian	−1419	−3146**
Some college	−10635**	−11012**
High school grad.	−14476**	−15485**
No high school	−20891**	−20892**
Married w/o children	−3879**	−5103**
Female head	−15815**	−17506**
Single person	−19599**	−21658**
Other household type	−6509**	−7734**
Rural residence	−4931**	−6725**
Scale Shift (middle 95% of population)		
Age	4595**	5008**
Age-squared	−41**	−50**
Black	−17244**	−26509**
Hispanic	−2503	−6017
Asian	4290	12705
Some college	−22809**	−47992**
High school grad.	−32675**	−54434**
No high school	−44457**	−65956**
Married w/o children	77	−9264**
Female head	−10269	−27272**
Single person	−32576**	−56791**
Other household type	−7535	−906
Rural residence	−12218**	−25760**
Skewness Shift (middle 95% of population)		
Age	−0.0417**	−0.0100
Age-squared	0.0005**	0.0002
Black	0.1127	−0.0682
Hispanic	0.2745**	0.1565**
Asian	−0.0383	0.1469
Some college	0.0655	−0.2775**
High school grad.	0.0934	−0.2027**
No high school	0.2742**	−0.1456**
Married w/o children	0.0890	−0.0272
Female head	0.5404**	0.3193**
Single person	0.2805**	−0.0331
Other household type	0.0164	0.1640**
Rural residence	0.0012	−0.0740

NOTE: Significance (** $p < .05$) is determined by 95% confidence interval based on 500 bootstrap replicates.

Only significant shifts are counted. For a covariate, in-sync signs in the three shifts indicate that the covariate exacerbates inequality; the larger the number of significant signs, the stronger the exacerbating effect becomes. Out-of-sync signs indicate that the covariate may increase between-group inequality while decreasing within-group inequality, or vice versa. The left panel of Table 7.8 for the income model shows that none of the covariates have in-sync effects on inequality in 1991, but many do in 2001. These in-sync covariates are education groups, household types (except female heads), and rural residence. The right panel shows the corresponding results from the log-income model. We see little contradiction in the overall evaluation. For example, for education groups, the pattern changes from out of sync in 1991 to in sync in 2001 in both models. Thus, American society in 2001 was more unequal and its social stratification more salient by education, marriage, presence of children, and rural residence than was the case a decade earlier.

In this example, we use the middle 95% population to calculate the shape-shift quantities. Researchers can design their own shape-shift definitions according to their research questions. It is possible to design corresponding shape shifts for the middle 99%, 98%, 90%, 80%, or 50% of the population. We leave this to our readers to undertake.

TABLE 7.8
Overall Evaluation of Covariates' Role in Inequality:
Synchronicity Patterns in Coefficients

Variable	Income Equation		Log-Income Equation	
	1991	2001	1991	2001
Age	+ + −	+ + −	+ + −	+ + 0
Age-squared	− − +	− − +	− − +	− − 0
Black	− − 0	− − 0	− − 0	− − 0
Hispanic	− 0 +	− 0 +	− 0 +	− 0 +
Asian	0 0 0	− 0 0	0 0 0	− 0 0
Some college	− − +	− − 0	− − 0	− − −
High school grad.	− − +	− − 0	− − 0	− − −
No high school	− − +	− − 0	− − +	− − −
Married w/o children	− 0 +	− − 0	− 0 0	− − 0
Female head	− 0 +	− − +	− 0 +	− − +
Single person	− − +	− − 0	− − +	− − 0
Other household type	− 0 0	− − 0	− 0 0	− 0 +
Rural residence	− − 0	− − 0	− − 0	− − 0

112

Summary

What are the sources of the persistent and widening income inequality in the recent decade? To address this research question, we apply the techniques developed in this book. We start with a descriptive analysis using the notion of quantiles introduced in Chapter 2. For income data, we discuss the issues of right-skewed distributions and top-coding and explain why and how the QRM can accommodate these features. The analyses follow the steps discussed in Chapters 3 through 6: defining and fitting models, assessing the goodness of fit, estimating the inference of parameters, making graphs of coefficients and their confidence intervals, and calculating location and shape shifts and their inferences. We describe the income and log-income models, paying special attention to the reconstructed raw-scale coefficients. Along with our description of the steps, we demonstrate the utility of the QRM techniques in addressing the research question through interpretations of the results. It is our hope that this systematic summarization of the application procedures will provide clear guidance for empirical research.

APPENDIX: STATA CODES

Data: d0.dta is a Stata system file prepared for the analysis.

I. Stata Codes for Analysis of Raw-Scale Income

Step 1: Goodness of Fit

```
* q0.do
* a full model
* raw-scale income in $1000
* OLS
* 19 quantiles

tempfile t

use d0

global X age age2 blk hsp asn scl hsg nhs mh fh sg ot rural

* centering covariates
sum $X
tokenize $X
  while "`1'"~="" {
    egen m=mean(`1')
    replace `1'=`1'-m
    drop m
    macro shift
  }
sum $X

forvalues k=1/2 {
reg cinc $X if year==`k'
}

forvalues i=1/19 {
local j=`i'/20
qreg cinc $X if year==1, q(`j') nolog
}

forvalues i=1/19 {
local j=`i'/20
qreg cinc $X if year==2, q(`j') nolog
}
```

Step 2: Simultaneous Quantile Regressions With 500 Replicates

```
* s0.do
* full model
* sreq 19 quaniles
* raw-scale income in $1000
* analysis for 2001

tempfile t
set matsize 400

global X age age2 blk hsp asn scl hsg nhs mh fh sg ot rural

use cinc $X year if year==2 using d0, clear
drop year

* centering covariates
sum $X
tokenize $X
  while "`1'"~="" {
    egen m=mean(`1')
    replace `1'=`1'-m
    drop m
    macro shift
}
sum $X

sqreg cinc $X, reps(500) q(.05 .10 .15 .20 .25 .30 .35 .40 .45 .50 .55 .60 .65
.70 .75 .80 .85 .90 .95)
mstore b, from(e(b))
mstore v, from(e(V))
keep age
keep if _n<11
save s0, replace
```

Step 3: Use Results From s0.do to Create Tables and Graphs

```
* s_m0.do
* matrix operation
* 13 covariates + cons
* graphs for beta's (19 QR)
* 500 bootstrap se
* analysis for 2001

* for black-white graphs
set scheme s2mono

set matsize 400

* 13 covariate + cons
local k=14
* k parameters for each of the 19 quantiles
local k1=`k'*19

use s0, clear

qui mstore b
qui mstore v

* 95%ci
* dimension `k' x 1

mat vv=vecdiag(v)
mat vv=vv'
```

```
svmat vv
mat drop vv
qui replace vv1=sqrt(vv1)
mkmat vv1 if _n<=`k1', mat(v)
drop vv1

mat b=b'
mat l=b-1.96*v
mat u=b+1.96*v

* 19 quantiles
mat
q=(.05\.10\.15\.20\.25\.30\.35\.40\.45\.50\.55\.60\.65\.70\.75\.80\.85\.90\.95)

* reorganize matrix by variable

forvalues j=1/`k' {
forvalues i=1/19 {
local l=`k'*(`i'-1)+`j'
mat x`j'q`i'=q[`i',1],b[`l',1],l[`l',1],u[`l',1],v[`l',1]
}
}

forvalues j=1/`k' {
mat x`j'=x`j'q1
forvalues i=2/19 {
mat x`j'=x`j'\x`j'q`i'
}
* q b l u v
mat list x`j', format(%8.3f)
svmat x`j'

mat a1=x`j'[1...,2]
mat a2=x`j'[1...,5]
mat xx`j'=q,a1,a2
* q b v


mat list xx`j', format(%8.3f)
mat drop a1 a2 xx`j'
}

* graphs using the same scale for categorical covariates
* use age, age-squared and constant as examples
* age
twoway rarea x13 x14 x11, color(gs14) || line x12 x11, lpattern(solid) yline(0,
lpattern(solid) lwidth(medthick)) ylabel(0 "0" 1 "1000" 2 "2000" 3 "3000")
ytitle(quantile coefficients for income ($)) xtitle(p) xlabel(0(.1)1)
legend(off)
graph export g0.ps, as(ps) logo(off) replace

* age2
twoway rarea x23 x24 x21, color(gs14) || line x22 x21, lpattern(solid) yline(0,
lstyle(foreground) lpattern(solid) lwidth(medthick)) xtitle(p) xlabel(0(.1)1)
legend(off)
graph export g2.ps, as(ps) logo(off) replace

* constant (the typical setting)
twoway rarea x143 x144 x141, color(gs14) || line x142 x141, lpattern(solid)
yline(0, lstyle(foreground) lpattern(solid) lwidth(medthick)) ylabel(0(20)120)
xlabel(0(.1)1) xtitle(p) legend(off)
graph export g14.ps, as(ps) logo(off) replace

drop x*
matrix drop _all
```

Step 4: Calculating Location and Shape Shifts

```
* e0.do
* full model
* raw-scale income in $1000
* bootstrap
* analysis for 2001

tempfile t

global X age age2 blk hsp asn scl hsg nhs mh fh sg ot rural

use cinc $X year if year==2 using d0, clear
drop year

* centering covariates
sum $X
tokenize $X
  while "`1'"~="" {
    egen m=mean(`1')
    replace `1'=`1'-m
    drop m
    macro shift
}
sum $X

save `t'

forvalues i=1/500 {
use `t', clear
bsample

qreg cinc $X, q(.025) nolog
mstore e, from(e(b))
keep if _n<11
keep age
save e0`i', replace
}
```

[Modify the codes of e0.do to make e1.do for the .5th quantile and e2.do for the .975th quantile]

```
* bs0.do
* location and shape shift quantities
* bootstrap confidence interval
* 3 quantiles (.025, .5, .975)

set matsize 800

* k= # of covariates + cons
local k=14
local k1=`k'-1

* initial
forvalues j=0/2 {
use e`j'1, clear
qui mstore e
mat ren e e`j'
}

forvalues j=0/2 {
forvalues i=2/500 {
use e`j'`i', clear
qui mstore e
```

```
mat e`j'=e`j'\e
mat drop e
}
}

forvalues j=0/2 {
qui svmat e`j'
}

* mean of estimate (point estimate)
* percentile-method (95% ci)
forvalues j=0/2 {
forvalues i=1/`k' {
pctile x=e`j''`i', nq(40)
sort x
qui gen x0=x if _n==20
qui gen x1=x if _n==1
qui gen x2=x if _n==39
egen em`j''`i'=max(x0)
egen el`j''`i'=max(x1)
egen eu`j''`i'=max(x2)
drop x x0 x1 x2
sum em`j''`i' el`j''`i' eu`j''`i'
}
}

* SCS scale shift
forvalues i=1/`k1' {
gen sc1s`i'=e2`i'-e0`i'
pctile x=sc1s`i', nq(40)
sort x
qui gen x0=x if _n==20
qui gen x1=x if _n==1
qui gen x2=x if _n==39
egen sc1sm`i'=max(x0)
egen sc1sl`i'=max(x1)
egen sc1su`i'=max(x2)
drop x x0 x1 x2
sum sc1sm`i' sc1sl`i' sc1su`i'
}

* SKS skewedness shift
* SKS e2(.975) - e1(.5) and e1(.5) - e0(.025)
* i for covariate, k for constant
forvalues i=1/`k1' {
gen nu=(e2`i'+e2`k'-e1`i'-e1`k')/(e2`k'-e1`k')
gen de=(e1`i'+e1`k'-e0`i'-e0`k')/(e1`k'-e0`k')
gen sk1s`i'=nu/de
drop nu de
pctile x=sk1s`i', nq(40)
sort x
qui gen x0=x if _n==20
qui gen x1=x if _n==1
qui gen x2=x if _n==39
egen sk1sm`i'=max(x0)
egen sk1sl`i'=max(x1)
egen sk1su`i'=max(x2)
drop x x0 x1 x2
sum sk1sm`i' sk1sl`i' sk1su`i'
}
```

II. Stata Codes for Analysis of Log Income

[Substitute raw-scale income with log-scale income, following Steps 1–3 on pages 113 to 115]

Step 4: Calculating Raw-Scale Location and Shape Shifts Based on Log-Income QRM

[Substitute raw-scale income with log-scale income in e0.do, e1.do, and e2.do]

```
set matsize 800

* k= # of covariates + cons
local k=14
local k1=`k'-1

* parameter matrix (e0 e1 e2)
* initial
forvalues j=0/2 {
use e`j'1, clear
qui mstore e
mat ren e e`j'
}

* 500 reps
forvalues j=0/2 {
forvalues i=2/500 {
use e`j'`i', clear
qui mstore e
mat e`j'=e`j'\e
mat drop e
}
}

* get log conditional quantile
forvalues j=0/2 {

* dimensions 500 x 14
* c`j'1 to c`j'13 are covariates
* c`j'14 constant

forvalues m=1/`k' {
mat c`j'`m'=e`j'[1...,`m']
}
forvalues m=1/`k1' {
mat c`j'`m'=c`j'`m'+c`j'`k'
}

mat c`j'=c`j'1
mat drop c`j'1
forvalues m=2/`k' {
mat c`j'=c`j',c`j'`m'
mat drop c`j'`m'
}

* transform log-scale conditional quantile to raw-scale conditinal quantile
* matrix to var
svmat c`j'
mat drop c`j'

forvalues m=1/`k' {
qui replace c`j'`m'=exp(c`j'`m')
}
```

```
forvalues m=1/`k1' {
qui replace c`j'`m'=c`j'`m'-c`j'`k'
}

* var to matrix
forvalues m=1/`k' {
mkmat c`j'`m', mat(e`j'`m')


}

mat e`j'=e`j'1
mat drop e`j'1
forvalues m=2/`k' {
mat e`j'=e`j',e`j'`m'
mat drop e`j'`m'
}
mstore e`j', from(e`j') replace
}

mat dir
keep age
keep if _n<11
save l-r, replace

****

* bs1.do
* bootstrap method
* location and shape shift quantities
* based on log-to-raw coeff

set matsize 800

* k= # of covariates + cons
local k=14
local k1=`k'-1

use l-r

forvalues j=0/2 {
qui mstore e`j'
qui svmat e`j'
}

* mean of estimate (point estimate)
* sd of estimates (se)
* percentile-method (95% ci)
forvalues j=0/2 {
forvalues i=1/`k' {
pctile x=e`j'`i', nq(40)
sort x
qui gen x0=x if _n==20
qui gen x1=x if _n==1
qui gen x2=x if _n==39
egen em`j'`i'=max(x0)
egen el`j'`i'=max(x1)
egen eu`j'`i'=max(x2)
drop x x0 x1 x2
sum em`j'`i' el`j'`i' eu`j'`i'
}
}

* SCS scale shift
forvalues i=1/`k1' {
```

```
gen sc1s`i'=e2`i'-e0`i'
pctile x=sc1s`i', nq(40)
sort x
qui gen x0=x if _n==20
qui gen x1=x if _n==1
qui gen x2=x if _n==39
egen sc1sm`i'=max(x0)


egen sc1sl`i'=max(x1)
egen sc1su`i'=max(x2)
drop x x0 x1 x2
sum sc1sm`i' sc1sl`i' sc1su`i'
}

* SKS skewedness shift
* SKS e2(.975) - e1(.5) and e1(.5) - e0(.025)
* i for covariate, k for constant
forvalues i=1/`k1' {
gen nu=(e2`i'+e2`k'-e1`i'-e1`k')/(e2`k'-e1`k')
gen de=(e1`i'+e1`k'-e0`i'-e0`k')/(e1`k'-e0`k')
gen sk1s`i'=nu/de
drop nu de
pctile x=sk1s`i', nq(40)
sort x
qui gen x0=x if _n==20
qui gen x1=x if _n==1
qui gen x2=x if _n==39
egen sk1sm`i'=max(x0)
egen sk1sl`i'=max(x1)
egen sk1su`i'=max(x2)
drop x x0 x1 x2
sum sk1sm`i' sk1sl`i' sk1su`i'
}
```

REFERENCES

Abreveya, J. (2001). The effects of demographics and maternal behavior on the distribution of birth oucomes. *Empirical Economics, 26,* 247–257.

Austin, P., Tu, J., Daly, P., & Alter, D. (2005). The use of quantile regression in health care research: A case study examining gender differences in the timeliness of thrombolytic therapy. *Statistics in Medicine, 24,* 791–816.

Bedi, A., & Edwards, J. (2002). The impact of school quality on earnings and educational returns—evidence from a low-income country. *Journal of Development Economics, 68,* 157–185.

Berry, W. D. (1993). *Understanding regression assumptions.* Newbury Park, CA: Sage Publications.

Berry, W. D., & Feldman, S. (1985). *Multiple regression in practice.* Beverly Hills, CA: Sage Publications.

Buchinsky, M. (1994). Changes in the U.S. wage structure 1963–1987: Application of quantile regression. *Econometrica, 62,* 405–458.

Budd, J. W., & McCall, B. P. (2001). The grocery stores wage distribution: A semi-parametric analysis of the role of retailing and labor market institutions. *Industrial and Labor Relations Review, 54, Extra Issue: Industry Studies of Wage Inequality,* 484–501.

Cade, B. S., Terrell, J. W., & Schroeder, R. L. (1999). Estimating effects of limiting factors with regression quantiles. *Ecology, 80,* 311–323.

Chamberlain, G. (1994). Quantile regression, censoring and the structure of wages. In C. Skins (Ed.), *Advances in Econometrics* (pp. 171–209). Cambridge, UK: Cambridge University Press.

Chay, K. Y., & Honore, B. E. (1998). Estimation of semiparametric censored regression models: An application to changes in black-white earnings inequality during the 1960s. *The Journal of Human Resources, 33,* 4–38.

Edgeworth, F. (1888). On a new method of reducing observations relating to several quantiles. *Philosophical Magazine, 25,* 184–191.

Efron, B. (1979). Bootstrap methods: Another look at the jackknife. *Annals of Statistics, 7,* 1–26.

Eide, E. R., & Showalter, M. H. (1999). Factors affecting the transmission of earnings across generations: A quantile regression approach. *The Journal of Human Resources, 34,* 253–267.

Eide, E. R, Showalter, M., & Sims, D. (2002). The effects of secondary school quality on the distribution of earnings. *Contemporary Economic Policy, 20,* 160–170.

Feiring, B. R. (1986). *Linear programming.* Beverly Hills, CA: Sage Publications.

Fortin, N. M., & Lemieux, T. (1998). Rank regressions, wage distributions, and the gender gap. *The Journal of Human Resources, 33,* 610–643.

Handcock, M. S., & Morris, M. (1999). *Relative distribution methods in the social sciences.* New York: Springer.

Hao, L. (2005, April). *Immigration and wealth inequality: A distributional approach.* Invited seminar at The Center for the Study of Wealth and Inequality, Columbia University.

Hao, L. (2006a, January). *Sources of wealth inequality: Analyzing conditional distribution.* Invited seminar at The Center for Advanced Social Science Research, New York University.

Hao, L. (2006b, May). *Sources of wealth inequality: Analyzing conditional location and shape shifts.* Paper presented at the Research Committee on Social Stratification and Mobility

122

(RC28) of the International Sociological Association (ISA) Spring meeting 2006 in Nijmegen, the Netherlands.

Kocherginsky, M., He, X., & Mu, Y. (2005). Practical confidence intervals for regression quantiles. *Journal of Computational and Graphical Statistics, 14,* 41–55.

Koenker, R. (1994). Confidence intervals for regression quantiles. In *Proceedings of the 5th Prague symposium on asymptotic statistics* (pp. 349–359). New York: Springer-Verlag.

Koenker, R. (2005). *Quantile regression.* Cambridge, UK: Cambridge University Press.

Koenker, R., & Bassett, Jr., G. (1978). Regression quantiles. *Econometrica, 46,* 33–50.

Koenker, R., & d'Orey, V. (1987). Computing regression quantiles. *Applied Statistics, 36,* 383–393.

Koenker, R., & Hallock, K. F. (2001). Quantile regression: An introduction. *Journal of Economic Perspectives, 15,* 143–156.

Koenker, R., & Machado, J. A. F. (1999). Goodness of fit and related inference processes for quantile regression. *Journal of Econometrics, 93,* 327–344.

Lemieux, T. (2006). Post-secondary education and increasing wage inequality. *Working Paper No. 12077.* Cambridge, MA: National Bureau of Economic Research.

Machado, J., & Mata, J. (2005). Counterfactual decomposition of changes in wage distributions using quantile regression. *Journal of Applied Econometrics, 20,* 445–465.

Manning, W. G. (1998). The logged dependent variable, heteroscedasticity, and the retransformation problem. *Journal of Health Economics, 17,* 283–295.

Melly, B. (2005). Decomposition of differences in distribution using quantile regression. *Labour Economics,12,* 577–590.

Mooney, C. Z. (1993). *Bootstrapping: A nonparametric approach to statistical inference.* Newbury Park, CA: Sage Publications

Scharf, F. S., Juanes, F., & Sutherland, M. (1989). Inferring ecological relationships from the edges of scatter diagrams: Comparison of regression techniques. *Ecology, 79,* 448–460.

Scheffé, H. (1959). *Analysis of variance.* New York: Wiley.

Schroeder, L. D. (1986). *Understanding regression analysis: An introductory guide.* Beverly Hills, CA: Sage Publications.

Shapiro, I., & Friedman, J. (2001). *Income tax rates and high-income taxpayers: How strong is the case for major rate reduction?* Washington, DC: Center for Budget and Policy Priorities.

U.S. Census Bureau. (2001). *U.S. Department of Commerce News.* (CB01–158). Washington, DC.

Wei, Y., Pere, A., Koenker, R., & He, X. (2006). Quantile regression methods for reference growth charts. *Statistics in Medicine, 25,* 1369–1382.

INDEX

124

ABOUT THE AUTHORS

Lingxin Hao (PhD, Sociology, 1990, University of Chicago) is a professor of sociology at The Johns Hopkins University. She was a 2002–2003 Visiting Scholar at the Russell Sage Foundation. Her areas of specialization include the family and public policy, social inequality, immigration, quantitative methods, and advanced statistics. The focus of her research is on the American family, emphasizing the effects of structural, institutional, and contextual forces in addition to individual and family factors. Her research tests hypotheses derived from sociological and economic theories using advanced statistical methods and large national survey data sets. Her articles have appeared in various journals, including *Sociological Methodology, Sociological Methods and Research, Quality and Quantity, American Journal of Sociology, Social Forces, Sociology of Education, Social Science Research,* and *International Migration Review.*

Daniel Q. Naiman (PhD, Mathematics, 1982, University of Illinois at Urbana-Champaign) is a professor in, and chair of, the Department of Applied Mathematics and Statistics at The Johns Hopkins University. He was elected as a Fellow of the Institute of Mathematical Statistics in 1997, and was an Erskine Fellow at the University of Canterbury in 2005. Much of his mathematical research has focused on geometric and computational methods for multiple testing. He has collaborated on papers applying statistics in a variety of areas: bioinformatics, econometrics, environmental health, genetics, hydrology, and microbiology. His articles have appeared in various journals, including *Annals of Statistics, Bioinformatics, Biometrika, Human Heredity, Journal of Multivariate Analysis, Journal of the American Statistical Association,* and *Science.*